KEYS TO INVESTING IN MUNICIPAL BONDS

Gary Strumeyer, M.B.A.

BARRON'S

© Copyright 1996 by Barron's Educational Series, Inc.

All rights reserved.
No part of this book may be reproduced in any form,
by photostat, microfilm, xerography, or any other means,
or incorporated into any information retrieval system,
electronic or mechanical, without the written permission
of the copyright owner.

All inquiries should be addressed to:
Barron's Educational Series, Inc.
250 Wireless Boulevard
Hauppauge, NY 11788

Library of Congress Catalog Card Number 96-2359

International Standard Book Number 0-8120-9515-4

Library of Congress Cataloging-in-Publication Data
Strumeyer, Gary.
     Keys to investing in municipal bonds / by Gary Strumeyer.
        p.   cm. — (Barron's business keys)
     Includes index.
     ISBN 0-8120-9515-4
     1. Municipal bonds. 2. Portfolio management. I. Title.
II. Series.
HG4726.S77   1996
332.63'233—dc20   96-2359
                                    CIP

PRINTED IN THE UNITED STATES OF AMERICA

98765432

CONTENTS

1

INTRODUCTION TO THE MUNICIPAL (TAX-EXEMPT) BOND MARKET

To those unfamiliar with the tax-exempt bond market, municipal bonds conjure up an image of a greedy old multimillionaire, sitting in his mansion, clipping tax-free coupons, and avoiding the taxes that we "little people" are obligated to pay. While there is no denying that municipal bonds are purchased by those of the highest wealth levels, their appeal is much broader. *One does not have to be a millionaire to enjoy the benefits of municipal bonds.* In fact, many middle class taxpayers find municipal bonds to be an integral part of their investment portfolios. For those looking to reduce their tax burden—not only the rich need tax relief—municipal bonds may be the only game left in town.

Using some basic arithmetic, one can ascertain whether municipal bonds should be considered as an investment vehicle. For example, an investor in the 35 percent tax bracket keeps only 65 percent (100 percent – 35 percent) of every dollar earned on a taxable investment, such as a certificate of deposit—CD. Therefore, a 5 percent CD yields an investor in the 35 percent bracket only 3.25 percent (5 percent × 65 percent) in true "after-tax dollars." A triple tax-free—exempt from federal, state, and local taxes—municipal bond yielding 4.25 percent involves an increase in income for this investor (a full 1 percent) because the investor gets to keep the full 4.25 percent. Remember, it is not the amount an investor earns but how much the investor retains after paying Uncle Sam!

1

This book was written to help demystify an obscure and misunderstood market that is often neglected by the financial press. Investors will learn about the overall economic and investing environment, the basic types of municipal bonds, and the workings and unique features of the municipal bond market. After reading this book, the investor should be equipped with all the knowledge needed to successfully purchase tax-exempt bonds, as well as manage a municipal bond portfolio. For anyone who currently pays taxes and has ever purchased a certificate of deposit (CD), this book is a must read!

2

WHAT ARE MUNICIPAL BONDS?

Municipal bonds are bonds issued by states and their political subdivisions: counties, cities, towns, school districts, and other governmental bodies.

When investors purchase municipal bonds, they are, in effect, lending money to these local governments in order to finance various public projects. For example, funds can be raised to build hospitals and schools and to repair the infrastructure.

What distinguishes municipal bonds from other fixed-income investments is the tax-exempt status of the interest paid by the municipality. Interest income received on municipal investments is not subject to federal taxes. In the vast majority of cases, states do not tax the interest income generated by bonds issued by that state or by any of its political subdivisions. For example, a New York State taxpayer who purchases any bond issued by New York State or any of its governmental bodies, such as counties, towns, school districts, etc., would not have to pay federal, state, or local taxes on the income produced by this bond. The interest is thus deemed to be triple tax free for the New York State resident purchasing "home-grown" bonds.

There are three general categories of municipal bonds: *general obligation bonds, revenue bonds,* and *pre-refunded bonds.*

- *General obligation bonds* (G-Os). These bonds are backed by the full faith and credit of the issuer. The bond's security is thus derived from the municipality's *taxing power.* Voter approval is necessary in order to issue G-O bonds.

3

- *Revenue bonds.* These bonds are secured by revenues derived from a specific project, such as user fees and rents. Examples of revenue bonds include: airport bonds, housing bonds, health care bonds, water and sewer bonds, and student loan bonds. Normally, no voter approval is needed in order to issue revenue bonds.
- *Prefunded bonds.* These are "old bonds" that have since been transformed into government-backed securities. They maintain a complex financial structure. Investors who devote the time to understand what prefunded bonds are all about, are rewarded with gilt-edged security.

In addition to these classifications we can break down municipal bonds by their unique financial characteristics as well:

- *Insured municipal bonds.* Municipal bond insurers guarantee the timely payment of interest and principal. In the event of a default on the part of the underlying issuer, a municipal insurer would step in, making interest and principal payments to the bondholder.
- *Zero coupon municipal bonds.* No periodic interest is paid on these bonds. The investor buys these bonds at a discount, a price less than face value, and at maturity receives the full face value, or par. The difference between the price paid and the face amount received at maturity is normally considered tax free.
- *Municipal notes.* Tax anticipation notes (TANs), revenue anticipation notes (RANs), tax and revenue anticipation notes (TRANs), and bond anticipation notes (BANs) are the most common types of municipal notes issued. They typically mature within one year and pay their full interest at maturity, unlike ordinary bonds that pay interest semiannually (twice a year).
- *Put bonds.* A put bond gives investors the right to tender, or relinquish, their bond at some specified

4

date at a specific price (normally par) prior to the bond's stated maturity date.

- *Variable-rate demand bond* (*lower floater*). This is a long-term bond that is transformed by a bond dealer into a short-term security. Interest rates are changed (float) on a daily, weekly, or monthly basis. Investors are given the right to tender the bonds at corresponding intervals. Major banks are often brought on board to guarantee the timely payment of interest and principal.
- *Super Sinkers*. These are associated primarily with single-family housing issues. By applying all funds received from mortgage repayments to the early retirement of these specific bonds, their average life is shortened significantly.
- *Certificates of participation* (*COPs*). These are bonds whose ultimate backing is derived from some form of lease payments.

The categories and characteristics of municipal bonds outlined above will be discussed in great depth in the following Keys.

3

INVESTING IN U.S. TREASURY SECURITIES

Treasury securities are IOUs that are backed by the full faith and credit of the U.S. government. They are issued by the federal government to raise money to help run the country. Investors are, in effect, lending the United States money with a promise of repayment on the maturity date. While Treasury securities are not considered municipal instruments, since they are issued by the federal, rather than state or local governments, they are nonetheless discussed in this book for two reasons:

1. Treasury securities are considered to be risk free (gilt-edged), *the standard by which the creditworthiness of all fixed-income vehicles are judged.* It must be noted, however, that in early 1996, Moody's Investors Service threatened a possible downgrade of U.S. government securities, due to the refusal by Congress to raise the debt ceiling. It seemed that this debt ceiling issue was being held hostage in a heated balanced budget negotiation between the president and Congress. The raising of the debt ceiling had become customary and an integral part of the running of the U.S. government. The refusal to do so threatened the government's ability to repay its financial obligations, that is, Treasury securities. While this threat never materialized, the mere mention of the possibility sent shock waves through the financial markets.

2. The yields on Treasury securities are used by virtually all fixed-income markets—domestic, as well as international—as a *benchmark*. Municipal bond

interest rates, for example, are continually being compared to that of Treasury securities to ascertain the risk/reward tradeoff. In other words, is the increased return on municipal bonds sufficient to compensate for the added, albeit minimal, additional risk?

Treasury securities are issued in the primary, or new issue, market through an auction process. Investors can subscribe to a Treasury auction directly through the Federal Reserve (Treasury Direct) without paying a commission charge, or through a brokerage house or bank with a minimal transaction fee tacked on. "Used" Treasuries can be purchased in the secondary market as well, exclusively from brokerage houses and banks. Interest received from Treasury securities, while taxable on a federal level, are generally exempt from state and local taxes, a real boon for residents of high income tax states, such as New York and California.

Based upon their maturities, Treasuries are classified as either Treasury bills (T-bills), Treasury notes (T-notes), or Treasury bonds (T-bonds).

Treasury Bills. Treasury bills mature in one year or less (they normally come in three-month, six-month, or one-year maturities) and are issued as *discount securities*. With a discount security, investor's receive no semiannual coupon interest. They pay less than face amount and at maturity receive the full face value, with the difference between the purchase price and redemption amount representing their interest. Three-month and six-month T-bills are auctioned off every Monday, with one-year bills auctioned off the third week of every month, usually on a Thursday. The interest rate on the bills, announced by the Treasury Department following the auction, is determined through market supply-and-demand forces. Understanding how T-bill yields are quoted is a little tricky, and thus requires a brief explanation.

Treasury bills are normally quoted in terms of a yield called the discount rate—not to be confused with the discount rate set by the Federal Reserve in conducting monetary policy. The discount rate, however, is an inaccurate gauge of the security's true return, since this rate assumes that the full face value is invested, rather than the discounted amount, and it is annualized using a 360-day year, rather than a 365-day year. By employing some mathematical wizardry, adjusting for both shortcomings, this discount rate is converted to what is known as a *bond equivalent yield*. The bond equivalent yield, always higher than the discount rate, is then used to compare T-bills to other non-discount (coupon-bearing) fixed-income instruments.

Treasury bills are among the most liquid of fixed-income instruments. Their yield quotes can be found in most business periodicals, such as *The New York Times* and *The Wall Street Journal*.

Treasury Notes. Treasury securities auctioned with maturities from two years to ten years are labeled Treasury notes (T-notes). They are generally issued in noncallable form. Unlike Treasury bills, T-notes—not to be confused with municipal notes—are issued at par, or full face amount, rather than at a discount, and pay interest every six months (semiannually). They are normally quoted on a dollar price basis in units of $\frac{1}{32}$; that is, 94-16 meaning 94 and $\frac{16}{32}$s, or 94½, or $945 for every $1,000 bond, with their price ultimately determined once again by market supply and demand forces. Like municipals, their return is quoted on a yield-to-maturity basis (readily comparable to other fixed-income instruments), so that there is no need to adjust this figure as in the case of T-bills. T-notes are auctioned by the Treasury on a considerably more staggered basis than T-bills.

Due to the generally upward sloping yield curve, where the longer the maturity, the higher the yield, (see Key 9), T-notes usually offer the investor higher returns than T-bills.

Treasury Bonds. Treasury bonds are almost identical to Treasury notes, except they have longer maturities. A Treasury security with a maturity of more than 10 years is referred to as a *bond*. They are so much alike that even the newspapers don't bother differentiating them when listing their price quotes. The most popular of Treasury bonds is the celebrated 30-year Treasury bond, considered the bellwether, or lead bond for all fixed-income securities. When it is reported that the "bond market is up," it is undoubtedly the 30-year Treasury bond that is being referred to. Due to its long maturity and thus unrivaled volatility, traders and other market professionals use the 30-year Treasury bond as a speculative trading vehicle. Neophyte investors are urged to use the 30-year Treasury bond solely as a market barometer, rather than as an investment vehicle. A 7- or 10-year Treasury security may offer the investor a comparable return with significantly less interest rate risk.

4

PROPERTIES OF FIXED-INCOME SECURITIES

When purchasing a bond, an investor is, in effect, lending money to the issuer of the security—the borrower. The issuer agrees to pay a specific amount of periodic interest, or steady payments, over the life of the instrument, and to return the borrowed funds at an agreed upon maturity date. The basic features of bonds (fixed-income instruments) include:

- *The issuer*—the party borrowing the funds through floating, or selling, a bond issue. Issuers of fixed income securities include: the U.S. federal government (Treasury bonds), domestic and foreign corporations (corporate bonds), and of course states and their political subdivisions (municipal bonds).
- *Coupon rate*—the stated rate of interest paid to the bondholder during the life of the bond. It is generally paid semiannually.
- *Maturity date*—the date on which the bond is paid off and the debt ceases to exist.
- *Par value*—the face amount of the bond upon which the interest payments are figured, such as par amount × coupon rate/2 = semiannual interest payments. It is the amount that is repaid on the maturity date.
- *Current yield*—yield calculated by dividing the coupon rate by the current price of the bond.
- *Yield to maturity*—the internal rate of return on any bond.

- *Call features*—agreements that give the issuer the right to redeem bonds on a given date or dates prior to maturity at some specified price.
- *Bond price*—the price, or market value, of a bond that one can determine, given the coupon rate, call features, maturity date, and yield to maturity, through a present value calculation.
- *Premium*—the amount by which the price of a bond *exceeds* its face value.
- *Discount*—the amount by which the price of a bond is *less* than its face value.
- *Sinking fund*—fund set aside by the issuer to retire, or call in, a certain amount of debt each year.

All the features listed above will be explained in greater detail in subsequent Keys.

5

THE TAX TREATMENT OF MUNICIPAL BONDS

Prior to delving into the intricacies of the tax law as it relates to municipal bonds, it is worth repeating a fundamental rule regarding the tax treatment of municipal bond interest: *The interest received from municipal bonds is free from federal taxation.* For almost eight decades following the installation of the U.S. income tax system, this exemption of municipal interest was considered a "divine right," based upon the landmark Supreme Court decision of *Pollock v. Farmers Loan and Trust Company.* This case codified the constitutional principal of reciprocal immunity: Since the states were prohibited from taxing the interest generated by federal securities, it was reasoned that the federal government should not tax interest on state obligations. In 1988, however, as a result of the Supreme Court's case of *South Carolina v. Baker* it was ruled that the tax exemption of municipal interest is not protected by the Constitution. While it did not by any means repeal the tax-exempt nature of municipal interest, the Supreme Court ruling did, however, open the possibility that someday this interest could become taxed if Congress so desires. Municipal bond interest is thus currently tax free only because our nation's lawmakers say it is.

Taxable Equivalent Yield. Municipal bond specialists often speak of this remarkable *taxable equivalent yield* as an apples-compared-to-apples formula that enables an investor to compare the yield on tax-exempt securities to comparable taxable bonds. The derivation of this formula is quite simple: for example, if an investor is in the 50 percent total marginal tax bracket, that investor gets to keep 50 percent of whatever he/she earns on a taxable investment, with the remaining 50 percent going to the federal, state, and local governments for tax payments. Mathematically, it can be stated:

taxable yield × (100% − marginal tax rate) = after-tax return

For example, a certificate of deposit yielding 5 percent provides an investor in the 50 percent marginal tax bracket a true after-tax return of 2.5 percent.

$$5\% \times (1.00 - .50) = 2.5\%$$

Employing some basic algebra, the above equation can be modified to:

taxable equivalent yield (taxable yield) =
tax-free yield (after-tax return) / (100% − marginal tax rate)

EXAMPLE:

A tax-free bond yielding 4 percent (.04) has a taxable equivalent yield for an investor in the 50 percent marginal tax bracket of 8 percent (4 percent / [1.00 − .50]). What this means is that 4 percent tax free is worth the same to this investor as 8 percent taxable. Why? Because if the investor was able to earn 8 percent on a taxable investment, 50 percent (4 percent of the 8 percent) would go toward taxes and the investor would keep the remaining 4 percent. Therefore, 8 percent taxable is the same as 4 percent tax free for this high tax bracketed individual or 8 percent is the taxable equivalent of 4 percent tax free. This formula is invaluable when comparing tax-exempt municipal bonds to alternative taxable investments. Investors must come equipped with their marginal tax bracket, usually obtained from their accountant or tax preparer, and the rest is simple.

State Tax Treatment of Municipal Bonds. As a rule, states that levy income taxes—some states, such as Florida, do not levy any income tax whatsoever—do indeed tax the interest generated by municipal bonds. However, the majority of these states do not tax the interest on bonds issued by that state or by any of its political subdivisions. For example, interest on a New

York City Municipal Water Authority bond would be exempt from both federal and state taxes—double tax free—for a New York State resident. Incidentally, for a resident of New York City, the interest generated by this bond would be exempt from local taxes as well (triple tax free for city residents), since localities generally treat tax-exempt income in a similar fashion as the state. It must be noted that several states such as Illinois tax the interest income on bonds issued by the state or any of its municipalities. For residents of these states, there is no advantage whatsoever to buying "home-grown" bonds.

Alternative Minimum Tax. The alternative minimum tax (AMT) is one of those esoteric parts of the tax code that only those affected by it take the time to learn about. Following the Tax Reform Act of 1986, many municipal investors were forced to find out what this AMT was all about.

What is the alternative minimum tax? In an attempt to penalize those with too many tax deductions and make these taxpayers (or avoiders) pay their fair share, the IRS created the alternative minimum tax (AMT). Basically, the AMT requires taxpayers to eliminate, or add back to taxable income, certain deductions that the tax code defines as "preference items," such as depletion allowances on oil and gas deals, casualty losses, real estate taxes, etc. Taxpayers must calculate their taxable income base in two ways:

- under the normal (non-AMT method) taxable income computation, with all deductions included; and
- under the alternative minimum tax method, adding back to taxable income all preference items (disallowed deductions).

Invariably the taxpayer must then pay the IRS, whichever is greater:

1. The taxable income figure generated under the non-AMT method, multiplied by the taxpayer's normal *effective* tax bracket—28 percent, 31 percent, 39 percent, etc.—or,

14

2. The taxable income figure calculated under the alternative minimum tax method, adding back disallowed deductions, multiplied by the prevailing AMT tax rate, that is, 26 percent, which is generally lower than the high income taxpayer's normal non-AMT tax bracket.

What the IRS is actually saying to those with a disproportionately large amount of deductions is: "Figure out your tax burden under normal circumstances, and then figure out your taxable income with those shelters, write-offs, and other deductions disallowed (added back in). We will give you a lower tax rate (AMT rate) to use in calculating your AMT income tax burden, and even a standard deduction. Now, pay, whichever is higher!"

The municipal bond market and the alternative minimum tax. Now that we understand the AMT, we can now see how the Tax Reform Act of 1986 thrust municipal bond buyers into the middle of this arcane tax law.

The Tax Reform Act prohibited the issuance of tax-free municipal bonds that funded a *private activity*. Interest generated by these private activity bonds was therefore no longer exempt from federal taxation. However, certain exceptions were permitted for various types of *qualified* private activity bonds, including qualified small issues, qualified mortgage bonds, etc. Interest on these qualified tax-exempt bonds issued after 1986, while remaining essentially tax exempt, must be included however, as a preference item when calculating the alternative minimum tax. Those investors who are currently, or think they may eventually be, in the AMT bracket, should avoid AMT bonds at all costs. For those in this unique bracket, buying an AMT bond would amount to buying a taxable bond.

A warning sign for possible AMT problems would be involvement in tax shelters and excessive deductions of all sorts. Investors should question their accountants or tax preparers to confirm their true tax status (AMT or non-AMT). The vast majority of U.S. taxpayers, however, need not be concerned with the AMT. Actually, only a very small percentage of taxpayers fall into this tax

15

bracket. For those who are not members of this exclusive club, AMT bonds may present an excellent buying opportunity. To compensate for the uncertainty surrounding their tax status, yields on these AMT bonds are often considerably higher than non-AMT bonds. Investing in AMT bonds is an effective way to increase portfolio returns without giving up credit quality.

Taxable Municipal Bonds. Following the Tax Reform Act of 1986, another unique municipal security—the taxable municipal bond—gained popularity. The act removed the tax-free status of municipal bonds issued to benefit private enterprises, or private purpose bonds, and limited the volume of issuance on other types of bonds; therefore, municipalities that wish to issue private purpose bonds or issue other types of bonds above the volume limit, may do so at taxable rates. A taxable municipal bond (an oxymoron!) is simply a municipal bond, issued by a state or its political subdivision, whose interest for whatever reason, such as nonqualified private purpose bond, or an issue that surpasses a volume cap on tax-free issuance—is not exempt from taxation. Taxable municipal bonds generate returns similar to other taxable instruments, such as corporate bonds.

6

UNDERSTANDING THE TIME VALUE OF MONEY

The concept of the time value of money, although difficult for the novice investor to comprehend, is an invaluable resource in understanding how bonds work. A careful study of this chapter will provide the neophyte investor with the basic tools in understanding how the price of a bond is calculated (see Key 7).

Future Value. Given a choice between receiving $100 today, or the same $100 one or two years down the road, a rational investor should take the money *now!* Assuming a hypothetical world where the only investment available is a one-year maturity bank CD (certificate of deposit) yielding 5 percent, the investor can take the $100 today, invest it at 5 percent for one year and at the end of this period realize $105 (original $100 plus $100 × 5 percent). The $105 can then be reinvested for an additional year at the same 5 percent yielding $110.25 ($105 plus $105 × 5 percent). Given a 5 percent investment interest rate, $100 today is worth $105 a year from now, and $110.25 two years from now. Therefore, it should make no difference to the investor whether he/she receives $100 today, $105 one year from now, or $110.25 in two years; a dollar received today is worth more than a dollar acquired any time after. Through the power of *compounding,* a sum of money invested today will continue to grow, since interest is earned not only on the original investment ($100) but on the interest so far accumulated. In financial terms, we can thus state: Given a 5 percent interest rate the *future value* of $100 in one year is $105, and $110.25 in two years. If this sum is then reinvested at 5 percent at the end of the third year, the future value will then become $115.76 ($110.25 plus $110.25 × 5 percent).

Consequently, the following basic formula can be used to compute the future value of a sum of money, given a stated interest rate:

Let I = stated interest rate;
  N = number of periods, such as years;
  FV = future value ($); and
  P = original sum to invest ($), or principal

Therefore:

$$FV = P (1 + I)^N$$

EXAMPLE:
An individual receives $1,000 as a settlement of a lawsuit. If the $1,000 is then invested in a financial instrument that yields 7 percent per annum, the future value of this sum will be $1,310.77, in four years.

I = .07 (7%)
N = 4 (years)
P = $1,000 (principal)
FV = $1,000 (1 + .07)^4
  = $1,310.77

In practice, few financial people actually use this formula. Rather, in this technologically sophisticated world, a financially equipped calculator, such as the Hewlett Packard, HP 12C, or the inexpensive Texas Instruments BA-35, has become the prime tool for computing.

Present Value. Present value is the logical reverse of future value. Given a stated rate of interest, how much is a specific amount in the future—future value—worth today (present value)? Given the hypothetical world where the only available investment is a one-year bank CD yielding 5 percent, we have seen how, through the power of *compounding,* $100 invested grows to $105 at the end of one year, $110.25 at the end of two years, and $115.76 by the end of the third year. We can now say that the present value of $105 received one year from now is

18

$100; the present value of $110.25 received in two years is also $100; and the present value of $115.76 obtained in three years is only $100, as well. Thus, individuals in this hypothetical world should not care whether they receive $100 today, $105 one year from now, $110.25 in two years, or $115.76 in three years, since, in present value terms, they are all equivalent.

The method of computing the present value of a sum, or sums, of money is known as *discounting,* which is, in effect, reversing the process of compounding. When discounting a future sum of money, or a series of future sums, one must answer the question: Given a specific interest rate, how much is that future sum or sums worth in today's dollars? With the help of a little basic algebra, the original formula presented in the future value discussion above can be reworked to obtain a new formula for calculating the present value:

Original formula: future value = present value $(1 + I)^N$
New formula: present value = future value $(1/[1 + I]^N)$

EXAMPLE:

An individual wins a $2,000,000 lottery, paid in annual installments of $100,000 a year for the next 20 years. Given a discount rate of 5 percent (5 percent was chosen because it approximates what individuals could earn on their funds over this time period), what is the present value of this string of cash flows?

$$I = .05 \ (5\%)$$
$$N = 1 \text{ through } 20 \text{ years}$$
$$FV = \$100,000 \text{ each year, for 20 years}$$
$$\text{present value} = \text{future value } (1/[1 + I]^N)$$

Present value = $100,000 (1/1 + .05) + $100,000 $(1/1 + .05)^2$
  + $100,000 $(1/1 + .05)^3$ + $100,000 $(1/1 + .05)^4$
  + $100,000 $(1/1 + .05)^5$, etc. = $1,246,221.03

From this example, it becomes obvious that two million dollars paid in installments over 20 years is really not worth anywhere near a true two million dollars. It should make no difference whatsoever to financially sophisticated lottery winners whether they receive $1,246,221.03 today or $2,000,000 based on the payment schedule illustrated above, since in present value terms, $1,246,221.03 today is the financial equivalent of $100,000 a year for 20 years. The key point to note is that the $100,000 to be received next year is actually not worth $100,000 but only $95,238 ($100,000 [1/1 + .05]), with the $100,000 received the following year worth even less, $90,703 ($100,000 [1/1 + .05]^2) (the present value of a sum of money decreases the later it is received), and so on. By adding up the individual present values, the total present value ($1,246,221.03) for the sequence of payments is calculated.

As seen by the above example, lottery winners most often receive far less than stated through the hype and promotions. This is not the end of the story, as out of this present value reduced winnings the Internal Revenue Service must receive its fair share. For an investor in the 45 percent marginal tax bracket, this brings the after-tax present value to a paltry $685,421. Thus, this $2,000,000 windfall is really worth only $685,421 in today's dollars after paying the appropriate taxes.

As with the compounding computations, discounting cash flows is normally done today utilizing some type of electronic calculator. By inputting the appropriate parameters, the computer will deliver the present value. Understanding the concepts presented is a necessary ingredient in learning how to calculate the price of a bond, which will be explained in the following Key.

7

BOND PRICES

Bond prices are normally quoted as a percentage of the bond's face, or par, value. For example, a price of 100 indicates that a bond is selling at 100 percent of its face value or $1,000 for a $1,000 bond. When a bond sells at 100 percent of its face value, we can say it is selling *at par*. If a bond is selling at a price greater than par, it is said to be trading at a *premium*. For example, a price of 105 means that the bond is selling at 105 percent of its face value, or $1,050 for every $1,000 bond. If a bond is selling at a price below par, it is said to be trading at a *discount*. For example, a price of 95 means that the bond is selling at 95 percent of its face value, or $950 for every $1,000 bond. Thus, we can see that a $1,000 bond can be purchased at an even $1,000, at *par,* for more than $1,000, at a *premium,* or for less than $1,000, at a *discount*. Although we are using a $1,000 bond in our examples for simplicity's sake, we must remember that minimum denominations for bonds currently issued is $5,000.

Changes in Bond Prices. In figuring changes in the price of a bond, market participants often speak of *points*. A single point is equal to 1 percent, or $10 per $1,000 bond. If the price of a bond, for example, falls from 95 (95 percent of face value) to 94 (94 percent of face value), we can say that the price of that bond decreased by one point, or $950 minus $940 is $10, or 1 percent of face value. In the same way, a price movement from 103 to 104 is an increase of one point.

The price of a bond can rise or fall for two distinct reasons:

1. a change in the credit quality of the issuer
2. a rise or fall in the level of interest rates

All things being equal, an improvement in a municipality's credit quality will lead to an increase in its bond's price, while a decline in the creditworthiness of an issuer will lead to a price decline in its bonds. For example, a vast improvement in a municipality's financial affairs, such as, the balancing of a previously unbalanced budget, and an accompanied upgrade by the rating agencies would lead to an increase in the value of the issuer's bonds. Conversely, a serious deterioration in an issuer's financial situation, such as the loss of a significant taxpayer, coupled with a downgrading by the rating agencies (see Key 46) would lead to a decline in the value of the issuer's bonds.

In addition, a rise in the level of interest rates will lead to a decrease in the price of a bond, while a decline in the level of interest rates will lead to the appreciation in the price of a bond. The understanding of this concept, called *interest rate risk,* is not nearly as intuitive as the former and thus requires a more detailed explanation:

EXAMPLE:
When interest rates go up, bond prices go down.
An investor purchases a $10,000 New York State 5 percent coupon rate bond maturing in 15 years at par (an even $10,000) in the new issue market. Six months later, the investor, considering the possible sale of the bond, wishes to ascertain the current value of the security. The investor finds out that the current market value for the bond is only 90—90 percent of face value, $900 per $1,000 bond, or, in this example, $9,000—even though New York State is no worse off financially than it was six months ago. The investor unfortunately fell victim to the dreaded interest rate risk! Why?

The interest rate (coupon rate) on New York State 15-year bonds *now* being issued, six months after the initial purchase, in the *new* sale market is 6 percent. No wonder no rational investor would purchase this "seasoned" issue at a 5 percent coupon rate when a new bond can be purchased at 6 percent. Therefore, in order to sell the 5 percent bond, the initial purchaser must offer it at less than par (*at a discount*) to entice purchasers to buy this lower rate bond. By buying the 5 percent rate bond at a price of 90 ($9,000 for the $10,000 face value), the purchaser receives less income each year. However, at maturity the purchaser will realize a gain of $1,000—at maturity the bondholder will receive the face value of $10,000—to make up for this shortfall of annual income. The combination of the 5 percent coupon rate and the $1,000 capital gain results in a 6 percent yield to maturity (YTM).

Interest rate risk, however, is a two-edged sword. A decline in interest rates will lead to an increase in the price of a bond.

EXAMPLE:
When interest rates go down, bond prices go up.

Using the prior example, we must consider the effect of falling interest rates on the $10,000 New York State 5 percent 15-year bond issued at par. Six months after the initial purchase, the investor finds that despite no improvement in New York State's financial condition, the bond, purchased at par ($10,000), is now worth 111—111 percent of face value, $1,110 per $1,000, or, in this example, $11,100. Here the investor had the pleasure of experiencing price appreciation caused by falling interest rates.

The interest rate (coupon rate) on New York State 15-year bonds now being issued, six months after the initial purchase, in the new sale market is 4 percent. All rational investors would just love to be able to buy the investor's seasoned issue—a 5 percent coupon rate—at par. Not so fast! The investor would be giving away this 5 percent coupon bond if he/she sold it at par because other investors are snapping up the 4 percent coupon bonds at par. Therefore, the investor demands a price of 111—a premium—to compensate for owning a municipal bond whose coupon rate is well above the prevailing rate on new issue bonds.

Calculating Bond Prices. It is now time to incorporate the material presented in the preceding Key (Understanding the Time Value of Money), and the above discussion, to figure out how we arrive at a bond's price. It may be helpful to review the preceding Key at this time.

Note: The price of a bond is equal to the present value of the future expected cash flows, with a yield to maturity used as the relevant rate (discount rate) to discount the cash flows.

Citing the above illustration of the falling bond price ($10,000 New York State 5 percent 15-year bond), we would like to show, using present value analysis, how we arrive at the price of a bond. Given a 5 percent coupon rate, a 15-year maturity date, and an environment where similar bonds are now being issued at 6 percent, what is the appropriate price of the New York State bond? In other words, what price would an investor have to pay for this bond to realize a 6 percent yield to maturity?

The price calculation is a three-step process:

1. *Determine the cash flows.* The cash flows generated by bonds generally include semiannual interest payments for the life of the bond, and the par value paid at maturity. They are as follows:

   > $250 semiannual interest payment
   > ($10,000 × 5 percent / 2 = $250)

   > $10,000 face value paid at maturity (end of 15 years)

2. *Determine the appropriate yield to maturity (YTM)* to use as a discount rate (required yield), in our example, 6 percent.

3. *Calculate the price* by taking the present value of $250 a period for 30 periods—15-year maturity multiplied by two semiannual payments each year—plus the present value of $10,000 in 15 years, all using 6 percent as the discount rate. As seen previously, the price is $900 per $1,000 bond or 90.

In our example of rising bond prices (as interest rates go down, bond prices go up), the relevant yield to maturity was 4 percent. Using this rate as the discount rate, with all other factors in the equation unchanged, we calculate a price of $1,110 per $1,000 bond or 1110.

The price of a bond is normally calculated using a financial calculator. By inputting the settlement date, coupon rate, maturity date, call dates, if any, and the yield to maturity, the calculator will display the bond's price.

Understanding how bond prices are calculated gives the investor the confidence to purchase premium (realizing, for instance, that a premium is not excessive commission for the unscrupulous broker) and discount bonds in addition to the simple par bond. By buying only par bonds, the investor is limiting the potential universe of bonds that can be purchased to new bonds issued at par, and older seasoned issues whose stated coupon rates coincidentally match the current market yield. By broadening the universe of potential bonds to include premiums and discounts, the investor is sure to significantly increase overall portfolio returns.

8

UNDERSTANDING BOND YIELDS

A quite successful technique used by an unscrupulous bond broker is that of quoting a somewhat irrelevant yield to the investor, that is, quoting the current yield, or coupon rate, rather than the yield to maturity, thereby fooling the investor into thinking that he/she is a getting a good deal. Therefore, it is essential for the investor to be able to distinguish between the various yields, and rates.

- *Coupon rate*—the stated interest rate printed on the bond, this is the rate used to figure how much interest the customer will receive, regardless of the price paid for the bond. For the typical municipal bond paying interest every six months, multiplying the coupon rate by the bond's par, or face, value, and then dividing this figure by two, provides the six-month interest payment. For example, to calculate the interest payment on a $10,000, 5 percent coupon rate bond, the investor would multiply the $10,000 face value by the 5.00 percent coupon rate, then divide by 2. The semiannual interest payment is thus $250.00.
- *Current yield*—this is simply the coupon rate divided by the price paid for the bond. For example, an investor purchasing a bond with a coupon rate of 8.00 percent, at a price of 107 ($1,070 for each $1,000 bond), is receiving a current yield of 7.48 percent or 8 percent divided by 107. This yield is not an accurate gauge of the investor's true return, as it does not take into account that, although the investor is paying $1,070 for the bond, he/she will only get a return of $1,000 at maturity. Quoting a

current yield to the customer is a common technique used by the unscrupulous broker to fool customers into thinking they are netting a superior return. While helpful to those investors concerned primarily with immediate income, the current yield should be ignored in favor of the yield to maturity when comparing yields on various financial instruments.

- *Yield to maturity*—this is a more complex yet more reliable measure of a security's true expected return. It takes into account the price appreciation of a discount bond, or the price depreciation of a premium bond. A technical definition would be the rate of interest that will discount all future cash flows—interest payments as well as principal repayment—to equal the price currently being paid for the bond (see Key 7). A simplified formula would be as follows:

  1. For a discount bond: YTM = current yield + price appreciation. For example: a 4 percent coupon bond maturing in 1999 is purchased at a price of 93, for a yield to maturity of 6.15 percent. Thus, the YTM is comprised of the current yield of 4.3 percent (4 percent/93) plus the 7 point price appreciation (100–93) adjusted for the time value of money.
  2. For a premium bond: YTM = current yield – price depreciation. For example: a 9 percent coupon bond maturing in 1999 is purchased at a price of 109, for a yield to maturity of 6.15 percent. Thus, the YTM is comprised of the current yield of 8.30 percent minus the 9 point price depreciation; while paying 109 for the bonds, $1,090 for every $1,000 bond, at maturity in 1999 the investor will only get back par or $1,000 for every $1,000 bond.

- *Yield to call*—this informs investors what their true yield would be if their bonds were called by the issuer prior to maturity. When a dealer quotes a yield to maturity on a premium bond that is callable, a price for the bonds must be calculated:

1. assuming the bonds will not be called;
2. assuming the bonds will be called.

The investor then pays the lower of the two prices. If there is more than one call, multiple prices must be calculated considering each potential call, thereby assuring the investor a minimum of the yield quoted. This conservative approach protects investors from paying large premiums, expecting them to be amortized over a long period till maturity, and having the bond called early, thereby losing their premium prematurely and lowering their true return (see Key 23).

- *After-tax yield*—this is applicable solely to municipal bonds and deals adjusting the YTM quoted on *discount bonds,* to reflect the fact that only the interest, and not the capital gains portion of the total return is tax free. For example, using the illustration above regarding the YTM on a discount bond (4 percent coupon rate, maturity 1999, and price 93), we see that while the yield to maturity is 6.15 percent, the "true" after-tax yield, assuming a 39 percent capital gains tax, is only 5.45 percent. This reflects the fact that only the 4 percent coupon portion of the bond's total YTM is tax free, with the capital gains share (100 – 93 = 7 points) subject to taxation, 39 percent.

9

THE YIELD CURVE

A bond's maturity date is a major determinant of its yield, or return. In analyzing why bond yields change as the maturity date changes (the term structure of interest rates), the *yield curve* is employed. It graphically depicts the relationship between the maturity of a bond and the interest rates offered on the bond. The following are the three basic shapes of a yield curve.

Upward Sloping

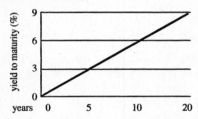

Longer maturity bonds pay a higher rate of interest than shorter bonds.

Flat

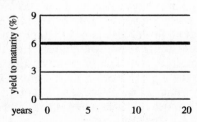

Longer maturity bonds pay the same or a similar rate of interest as shorter bonds.

Downward Sloping

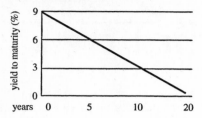

Longer maturity bonds pay a lower rate of interest than shorter bonds.

In explaining the derivation of various yield curve structures, economists employ several theories:

- liquidity preference theory
- expectation hypothesis
- segmented market hypothesis

Liquidity Preference Theory. It is most common for the bond market to experience an upward sloping yield curve, where investors are compensated in the form of a higher yield for committing their funds for an extended period of time. Since, all things being equal, having one's funds liquid—readily convertible to cash—is preferable over long-term investments (not readily convertible to cash), the market must pay some yield premium to induce investors to lend their funds for a protracted period. Furthermore, investors are often against heavy fluctuations in their securities' market value. Since longer maturity bonds are more volatile and riskier than short-term issues, higher returns must be offered. While doing a somewhat adequate job in explaining the customary upward sloping curve, this theory does not explain the appearance of the flat and downward sloping curves, and is therefore incomplete. The liquidity hypothesis is most valuable when it supplements the observations of the expectation hypothesis.

Expectation Hypothesis. Under the expectation hypothesis, long-term interest rates will be determined by an average of current short-term rates and *anticipated* short-term rates—anticipated by both lenders and borrowers—that are expected to prevail over the period in question. This equilibrium long-term rate should make investors and borrowers indifferent between lending or borrowing for a long period, or dealing in a series of short-term transactions.

EXAMPLE:

Assume an investor has a choice of lending funds for either one or two years. On the other side of the transaction, the issuer can borrow funds for either one or two years as well.

Assumption:
- current one-year interest rate of 4 percent
- expected (by both lender and borrower) one-year interest rate one year from now of 6 percent
- equilibrium two-year rate would be 5 percent, the average of 6 percent and 4 percent

Both the investor and the issuer would be indifferent between lending or borrowing funds for two years at 5 percent (a single two-period transaction), or for the first year at 4 percent, and the following year at the expected 6 percent.

Thus, the long-term, two-year rate is an average of the current one-year rate and the predicted two-year rate. While this two-period example is used for the sake of simplicity, the expectation hypothesis is applicable to a longer time frame as well. Any long-term rate is made up of the average of the prevailing short-term rate and the anticipated future short-term rates that will prevail over the applicable time frame. For example, the yield on a five-year bond is made up of the average of the current one-year rate and the anticipated one-year rate that will prevail in two years, three years, four years, and five years.

The expectation hypothesis can be used to explain the various shapes of the the yield curve:

- *Flat curve.* A flat yield curve comes about when the *expected* short-term rates are foreseen to remain about the same in the long run.

- *Upward sloping curve.* An upward sloping yield curve is derived when *expected* short-term rates are higher than *current* short-term rates.
- *Downward sloping curve.* A downward sloping yield curve is derived when *expected* short-term rates are lower than *current* short-term rates.

Market Segmentation Hypothesis. This theory assumes that lenders and borrowers are forced into certain segments of the yield curve, that is, some investors are forced to invest short term, while some issuers are forced to borrow short term as well. Therefore, the segmentation of borrowers and lenders creates a supply and demand tug of war for specific maturities, resulting in yields that are born out of this interplay. In the municipal bond market, for example, school districts often find it necessary to borrow funds short term to meet seasonal requirements. Bank portfolios are often the buyers of these school district notes. Therefore, according to this theory, the equilibrium interest rate on the short-term school district debt will be determined by the supply and demand of these two segmented market participants.

While none of the above-mentioned theories can by themselves fully explain the term structure of interest rates, combining these various theories will lead to a better understanding of this highly complex topic.

10

MACROECONOMICS 101

Prior to investing in any financial vehicle, it is essential that the investor understand the economic environment. Macroeconomics deals with the workings of the overall economy, including such topics as unemployment, inflation, the budget deficit, and foreign trade. Microeconomics, the other economic discipline, deals with narrower issues such as how, what, and at what price, products are produced by firms, supply and demand, etc. Just as cyclical changes in the economy will influence the performance of stocks, or equities, so too will these changes affect fixed-income securities. This effect will manifest itself in two ways:

1. *Credit risk.* A poorly performing national economy can affect the economic well-being of states and their political subdivisions, and ultimately the credit quality of both revenue and general obligation municipal bonds.
2. *Interest rate risk.* A change in the overall level of interest rates will have a profound effect on municipal bond prices (see Key 7). Understanding the economic variables associated with interest rate movements is thus critical in effectively managing one's municipal bond portfolio (see Key 48).

The following concepts are invaluable in understanding the workings of the nation's economy:

- *Gross Domestic Product (GDP)*—the sum of all goods and services produced within our nation's borders in a given year. By following the growth, or decline in the GDP, economists attempt to gauge the nation's economic well-being.

- *Budget deficit*—insufficiency that occurs when the government spends more in a given year than it receives in taxes and other revenues. It is the total dollar amount that spending exceeds revenue (see Key 14).
- *National debt*—the cumulative total of a nation's continued budget deficits. It is the total dollar amount of the money borrowed by the government and owed to the country's domestic and foreign creditors (see Key 14).
- *Unemployment*—state that occurs when people looking for jobs are unable to find them. Each month the Bureau of Labor Statistics (BLS) releases the nation's unemployment rate, which is the number of people looking for jobs as a percentage of the nation's labor force.
- *Inflation*—the upward trend of prices. By following such indices as the Consumer Price Index (CPI) and the GDP deflator, the government attempts to estimate the trend in the nation's prices. Remember, inflation is the archenemy of bonds, since any increase in prices hurts all investors receiving a *fixed income* (see Key 13).

Currently our government's policy goals involve sustaining economic growth, the continued control of inflation, and reductions in the nation's chronic budget deficit. The tools that are used to meet these economic objectives are fiscal policy and monetary policy (see Keys 11 and 12 respectively). The government's ultimate success in realizing these policy goals will have a profound effect on the municipal bond market.

11

FISCAL POLICY

Fiscal policy is one of the two general tools that the government uses to influence the total demand for goods and services, and ultimately economic growth and well-being. Monetary policy is the other.

Fiscal policy involves the use of government spending and/or taxation by the president and Congress to control the overall demand for goods and services by consumers, investors in physical assets, and the government. In more technical terms, the demand for goods and services is referred to as *aggregate demand*. Aggregate demand is thus equal to consumption (C) + investment (I) + government spending (G). This is a simplification of the full formula because the effects of foreign trade are being ignored. The following is a brief explanation of how fiscal policy is employed to expand economic activity during a recession, and slow the economy down during a boom period.

Expansionary Fiscal Policy. If the economy is mired in a recession the government could:

- cut marginal tax rates, thereby putting more money in the hands of consumers, who, hopefully, would spend a portion of this windfall (and save the difference). This spending would multiply throughout the economy, increasing aggregate demand and spurring economic activity. This multiplier effect is based on the concept that one person's spending is another person's income. When this income is received, a portion will, in turn, be spent as well. Thus, the initial spending injection will continue to multiply as income is received and ultimately spent by a series of consumers, and/or

- increase direct government spending on such things as the building of bridges and schools, military expenditures, and other government programs. This spending would directly affect aggregate demand through the government variable and would similarly stimulate a multiplier effect, increasing economic activity as well.

Contractionary Fiscal Policy. If the economy is booming and fueling excessive *demand pull inflation* (see Key 13), the government could:

- raise marginal tax rates, in effect, pulling money out of the hands of consumers, stimulating a reversal of the multiplier effect. This would lead to a decrease in aggregate demand, slowing down economic growth, and ultimately checking the inflationary spiral,

and/or

- decrease direct government spending on such things as infrastructure projects, military spending, etc., lowering the aggregate demand directly through less government spending. By experiencing less overall demand in the economy, a slowdown would again be initiated, ultimately keeping inflation in check.

Problems with the Implementation of Fiscal Policy. During periods when the federal government wants to redress a chronic budget deficit situation, fiscal policy is often rendered significantly less effective as a tool to increase economic activity. Why?

As previously mentioned, a budget deficit occurs when the government is spending more than it is receiving from taxes and other forms of revenue. The implementation of an expansionary fiscal policy to stimulate a recessionary economy involves either increased spending and/or a decrease in tax revenue. Both of these remedies involve exacerbating a budget deficit situation. As a result, the government must become increasingly reliant on its second policy tool, namely monetary policy (see Key 12).

12

MONETARY POLICY

Monetary policy involves the controlling of the nation's money supply and short-term interest rates. It is administered by the Federal Reserve Bank (the Fed), which can be viewed as the nation's inflation police. By effectively stabilizing inflationary pressures, the economy is thought to be better able to sustain economic growth, since the distortions created by inflation are eliminated. Some Federal Reserve economists go so far as to say that their job will not truly be over until inflation is no longer contemplated in the planning of the average citizen.

The Federal Reserve Bank was established in 1913 as the nation's central bank. Due to the geographic enormity of our country, there are 12 regional Federal Reserve banks dispersed throughout the nation, each with its own president.

The Fed is run by a seven-member Board of Governors, each of whom is nominated by the president and confirmed by the Senate for a 14-year term. One of these governors is designated by the president as chairman. The chairman wields enormous power and is considered one of the most powerful individuals in the world. Much controversy exists about the apolitical nature of this body, since members are not elected by the people. On one hand, this enables the Fed leaders to forego political factors and concentrate on employing the policy that they believe will best serve the country. On the other hand, these nonelected officials with no constituency influence the economic lives of millions of U.S. citizens without being directly answerable to those citizens.

The key decision-making body in the Federal Reserve system is the Federal Open Market Committee (FOMC), which is comprised of the seven-member Board of

Governors, in addition to five of the twelve regional presidents. The presidents each take turns serving on this committee, except for the president of the New York Federal Reserve Bank, who is a permanent member.

The Federal Reserve uses several policy tools to control short-term interest rates, to a lesser degree the money supply, and ultimately, economic activity.

Policy Tools of the Federal Reserve.

1. *Reserve requirement ratio.* Banks are required to keep a certain percent of all deposit liabilities on hand in the form of reserves, with the residual funds often loaned out to consumers and businesses. By altering the reserve requirement, the Fed can affect the banks' lending practices and, ultimately, economic activity. To stimulate economic activity, for example, the Federal Reserve can lower the *reserve requirement ratio,* thereby increasing loanable funds that would then circulate throughout the economy. Increasing this ratio would have exactly the opposite effect, pulling loanable funds out of the system, reducing economic activity. It must be noted, however, that varying the reserve requirement ratio is seldom employed as a policy tool.

2. *Open market operations.* This method is used most often by the Federal Reserve to control monetary policy. It involves the purchasing or selling of government securities (often on a temporary basis) to inject or remove reserves (money) from the banking system. A simplified representation is as follows:

   Fed wishes to slow down the economy. The Federal Reserve sells Treasury securities from its portfolio of U.S. government securities → receives check from Treasury dealer drawn on a commercial bank → reduces the amount of reserves in the banking system → reduction in money supply → upward pressure on federal funds rate (rate charged on overnight loans between banks) → slowdown in economic activity as consumers and businesses adjust spending to reflect higher borrowing costs.

Fed wishes to stimulate the economy. The Federal Reserve purchases U.S. government securities from Treasury dealers → sends check to the dealer firm in payment for the purchased bonds → increases the amount of reserves in the banking system → increase in the money supply → lowering the federal funds rate → stimulating economic activity as consumers and businesses respond to lower borrowing costs.

3. *Discount rate.* This is the rate charged by the Federal Reserve for loans to member banks. Since borrowing from the Fed is a privilege, and not a normal practice of banks, a change in the discount rate is seen as largely symbolic. By lowering the discount rate, for example, the Federal Reserve may be signaling the market that it is seeking lower interest rates.

13

INFLATION

Inflation involves a rise in the overall level of prices. Deflation, the opposite of inflation, entails falling prices. Economists attempt to track changes in the general level of prices by following various indices over a set time period. An index is used to characterize a set of data, which is a surrogate for the real thing. The most widely tracked index measuring inflation in the United States is the Consumer Price Index (CPI), which follows the cost of buying a typical "basket of goods" over a designated time period.

The basket of goods is made up of the prices of such things as food, clothing, and housing—364 separate classes of goods and services, weighted by their economic importance to the household. By following the trend in the CPI, economists attempt to ascertain what is happening to the prices of the things that the average American family is buying.

Economists compare the current CPI to a base period to arrive at some percentage change over the term. This percentage change is what is normally quoted in business periodicals and on radio and television reports when referring to inflation increases. For example, when it was reported that inflation rose 3 percent in 1994, it is a strong possibility that what was being reported was a 3 percent change in the CPI from base year 1993 to 1994. In addition to the Consumer Price Index, economists follow other inflation indices as well, including but not limited to, the Producer Price Index (PPI), which measures prices on the wholesale level, and the GDP deflator, which like the CPI, tracks prices on the consumer level.

Causes of Inflation. While it is difficult to identify the exact cause of inflation in a particular period, economists nonetheless attempt to classify inflation into three basic causal groups: *demand pull, cost push,* and *inertial inflation.*

- *Demand pull inflation.* Demand pull inflation occurs when aggregate demand—what consumers, investors, and the government want and are able to buy—rises more rapidly than what can be provided by firms that produce goods and/or supply services. In other words, too much demand is chasing too little supply, thus bidding up prices on the relatively scarce goods and services. Wages, a major component of a firm's cost structure, are bid up as well, since workers are hired and redeployed to meet this excessive demand, further exacerbating the inflationary trend.

- *Cost push inflation.* Economists were at a loss to describe a bout of inflation that occurred during a period of weak demand and high unemployment, when prices continued to rise while demand was weak. This phenomenon, which would eventually become known as cost push inflation, had little to do with the demand side of the equation, or spending of consumers, the government, or industry. Rather, it involved an increase in the cost of the factors of production, such as raw materials and wages. As the prices of the inputs into the production process are raised, producers are often forced to pass along the increases in the form of higher prices to the consumer. For example, in the late 1970s the Arab oil embargo led to a major increase in the price of oil, a primary input to the production process. This cost push shock was the driving force in the rampant inflation of that period.

- *Inertial inflation.* This involves the expectations that people and businesses have regarding future inflation and the way they react to these expectations in their day-to-day decision-making, such as building inflationary assumptions into contracts and cost-of-living increases. Thus, inflation may become a self-fulfilling prophecy as individuals and firms react to their expectations. Through aggressive monetary policy (see Key 12), the Federal Reserve strives to remove the inflationary element from the planning of the average U.S. citizen.

Severity of Inflation. Economists classify inflation as either moderate, galloping, or hyperinflation, according to its severity.

- *Moderate inflation.* This involves a predictable, steady, upward movement in prices, allowing firms and individuals alike to plan effectively, that is, to enter into contracts, take out mortgages, etc., with some assurance that prices will not rise excessively. While this form of inflation is palatable for most, some at the Federal Reserve feel that any inflation is too much inflation.

- *Galloping inflation.* This involves inflation in the double digits or above, leading people to hold as little cash as possible, in favor of holding physical assets such as land or gold, or similar properties, with money worth less and less from one day to the next. Although the interactions between borrowers and lenders (as well as among other economic participants) are distorted, that is, lenders are repaid by borrowers in dollars that are now worth considerably less, nations most often survive bouts of galloping inflation.

- *Hyperinflation.* This involves inflation that is running at astronomical rates, such as 1,000 to 1,000,000 percent. This form of inflation is fear-inspiring, since it can lead to the downfall of a country. According to historians, the hyperinflation prevalent in Germany in the early 1920s contributed to the rise of Adolf Hitler.

Inflation tends to reward borrowers at the expense of lenders. An unexpected bout of inflation can leave lenders in an unfortunate position, since they are repaid by borrowers with inflationary depreciated dollars, dollars that are worth considerably less than when first lent out. For example, those who took long-term mortgages in the 1960s found themselves in the enviable position of repaying lenders with ease. The galloping inflation of the late 1970s raised wages and incomes while the amount borrowed remained fixed, resulting in the real cost of the mortgage payments declining precipitously. The losers in this zero-sum game were the lenders—banks and savings and loans—that were repaid in dollars that were worth considerably less in real terms than when initially lent. In economic terms, inflation redistributed wealth in an arbitrary fashion that, in this case, benefited borrowers immensely.

14

THE BUDGET DEFICIT AND THE NATIONAL DEBT

While many citizens who were polled in late 1995 regarding the ills facing the nation's economy named the budget deficit as one of the country's major economic problems, few truly understand the consequences of this concept. A basic review of the budget deficit will help the investor better understand the workings of the economy, its effect on interest rates, and ultimately, on bond prices.

A budget deficit occurs each fiscal year when the nation spends more than it receives in taxes and other revenue. This shortfall must be made up by public borrowing. The national debt is the cumulative total of all budget deficits that have occurred over time, and the total of all funds borrowed and owed to the investing public. This concept can be compared to an individual earning $40,000 in 1994 and spending $50,000; a $10,000 budget deficit is thus created. Assuming that an identical earning and spending pattern had been in effect for the previous nine years as well, the individual's national debt would be $100,000, or $10,000 a year for ten years. A continuing pattern of similar earning and spending will undoubtedly lead to dire consequences, such as bankruptcy, for this financially imprudent individual. Thankfully for our nation, the comparison ends here. Continued budget deficits will *not* lead to the bankruptcy of the United States. Fortunately, our nation has deeper pockets than the average individual and can continue to "print money" to meet its financial obligations. This printing of money, however, does not come without cost. In many scenarios, excessive spending and the printing of money that can accompany it can lead to high inflation. In addition, budget deficits may cause other serious economic ills for the debtor country.

The Evils of Budget Deficits. While chronic budget deficits will not lead to the ruin of the country, there are some quite unhealthy ramifications when a government spends more each year than it is receiving in taxes and other revenue. These evils include: the *crowding-out effect, reliance on external debt, and the displacement of capital.*

The Crowding-Out Effect. The crowding-out effect manifests itself in two ways; increased competition for a finite pool of investment dollars, and tighter monetary policy.

Increased competition. By spending more each year than it is receiving in revenue, the federal government is forced into the capital markets to borrow the deficiency from the public. In effect, the government is competing with corporations, which must also borrow for their sundry needs, such as capital projects, for a fixed pool of funds that investors earmark to be lent to borrowers. This competition leads to rising interest rates (the price of money), thus raising the cost of doing business for firms that need to borrow. For example, without any competition from the government, a blue chip corporation, such as IBM, may borrow money for five years at 6 percent. Along comes the federal government with a need to borrow money for five years as well. This increased competition forces IBM to raise the interest it pays to 7 percent. Projects that were feasible under a lower interest rate environment may become prohibitive when factoring the cost of these higher interest rate payments. Private investment is therefore "crowded out" by the federal government borrowing.

Tighter monetary policy. By spending more than it is receiving each year, the federal government is, in effect, increasing aggregate demand—the total demand for goods and services—and ultimately economic growth (see Key 12). The Federal Reserve (the Fed) may judge this increase in economic growth as inflationary and apply the brakes to the economy through restrictive monetary policy, thus raising interest rates. Our nation's inflation police (the Fed), in attempting to offset the economic expansion caused by excessive government spending, raises interest rates, hoping to reduce the spending of others, such as corporate borrowers. Once again, corporate borrowers are being crowded out of the market by deficit spending.

Excessive budget deficit spending → increased economic growth → increased inflationary expectations → tight monetary policy → higher borrowing costs for corporations → reduced corporate investment → crowding out

Reliance on External Debt. External debt is created when a nation begins borrowing from foreigners rather than solely from its own citizens, which is called internal debt. Excessive internal borrowing, while somewhat troublesome, is not nearly as disturbing since, with internal borrowing, the country, in effect, owes money to itself. External debt leads to dollars falling into the hands of foreign citizens and central banks. If these foreign owners for whatever reason seek to dump U.S. dollars, the U.S. currency may then be devalued.

Displacement of Capital. As the government continues to run enormous deficits, U.S. citizens accumulate large holdings of government bonds. Rather than investing in *equities* (stocks) and other forms of direct ownership, investors find themselves lending immense sums to the federal government by purchasing Treasury securities. The result is fewer funds available to corporations to finance expansion, and a subsequent decline in economic growth and standards of living.

15

ECONOMIC VARIABLES AND STATISTICS INFLUENCING THE BOND MARKET

It's 8:30 A.M. in a Wall Street bond trading room. The Bureau of Labor Statistics has just released the latest employment numbers. The unemployment rate was up to 6 percent, the highest level in the past three years. Only 50,000 non-farm jobs were created, far below what was expected by most economists. A thunderous roar of elation emerges from the traders. What kind of perverse market views with happiness a weak economy and its accompanying high jobless rates? The bond market! Why?

An increase in the level of unemployment is one of many indications of a weak economy. All things being equal, a weakening economy will lead to falling interest rates (see below). When interest rates fall, bond prices rise (see Key 7). Any economic statistics that lead traders and economists to believe that interest rates are going to fall are therefore beneficial to the fixed-income market. Conversely, any variables that lead to an upward movement of interest rates are negative for the bond market. The economic statistics affecting the bond market can be classified into two general categories: those involving economic strength and weakness, and those involved in predicting inflationary trends. Remember, inflation is the archenemy of bonds.

Economic Strength and Weakness. Economic statistics released by the government, indicating the relative strength or weakness of the economy, include but are not limited to:

1. *Gross Domestic Product*—the sum of all goods and services produced within our nation's borders
2. *Unemployment rate*—the percentage of people unsuccessfully seeking employment
3. *Non-farm payroll*—the number of non-farm jobs created in a particular month
4. *Retail sales*—the aggregate amount of retail items sold in a particular month

Economic statistics showing greater economic strength than expected—the absolute number is not nearly as important as the number compared with Wall Street's consensus forecast or expectations—often leads traders to the following conclusions:

stronger than expected economy → Federal Reserve implementing restrictive monetary policy → raising the federal funds rate → leading to higher overall interest rates (but it must be noted that, under certain market conditions, an increase in the federal funds rate may actually lead to longer term rates falling as the Fed displays its diligence in fighting inflation) → lower bond prices, and/or

stronger than expected economy → increased demand pressures, where consumers want to purchase more, thus bidding up prices → inflation, the bonds' archenemy → lower bond prices.

An economic statistic displaying a weaker than expected economy often leads traders to the following conclusions:

weaker than expected economy → Federal Reserve loosening monetary policy → lowering the federal funds rate → leading to lower overall interest rates → higher bond prices, and/or

weaker than expected economy → decreased demand pressures → less inflation or deflation → higher bond prices.

Inflationary Trends. Economic statistics released by the government evidencing an inflationary or deflationary scenario include, but are not limited to, the following:

1. *Consumer Price Index* *(CPI)*—an index that attempts to gauge price movements on the retail level in the economy by tracking some hypothetical basket of goods over time (see Key 13).
2. *Producer Price Index* *(PPI)*—an index that attempts to gauge price movements on the whole-sale level in the economy by tracking some hypothetical basket of goods over time.
3. *Capacity utilization*—a percentage of capacity at which factories are operating. The greater the percentage, the closer the nation's industry is moving toward full capacity. The higher this figure, 90 percent, for instance, the greater the likelihood that firms will raise prices.

Economic statistics evidencing higher inflation lead traders directly to the following conclusion:

higher inflation indicators → higher future inflation rates → Federal Reserve implementing restrictive monetary policy (see Key 12) → raising Fed funds rate → higher overall level of interest rates → lower bond prices, and/or

higher inflation indicators → higher future inflation rates → directly leading to lower bond prices.

Economic statistics evidencing lessening inflation (or deflation) lead traders to the following conclusions:

lower inflation indicators → lower future inflation rates → Federal Reserve implementing easy monetary policy → lowering Fed funds rate → lower overall level of interest rates → higher bond prices, and/or

lower inflation indicators → lower anticipated inflation rate → directly leading to higher bond prices.

It can now be seen why bond traders who maintain considerable inventories of bonds are not necessarily dreadful human beings who enjoy the misery of others, but pragmatists driven by the dynamics of the bond market. All things being equal, bond prices rise when the economy displays weakness as well as low inflation.

16

CUSTOMER CONFIRMATION

Following the sale or purchase of any municipal security, the dealer is required to remit a confirmation verifying that a trade was consummated. Municipal bond confirmations must contain the following information:

1. *A line confirming the sale or purchase of the bonds,* for example: As principal we confirm our sale to you.
2. *Trade date*—the date the transaction is initiated and confirmed.
3. *Settlement date*—the date on which the bonds must be paid for. Unless otherwise specified, settlement in the municipal market is three business days following the trade date (Trade + 3, T+3).
4. *Par value*—the face value of bonds; the amount received at maturity.
5. *Coupon rate*—rate used to calculate the bonds' periodic interest payments.
6. *Maturity date*—the date funds are returned to the investor and obligation ceases to exist.
7. *Price* (see Key 7)
8. *Yield to maturity* (see Key 8)
9. *The Committee Uniform Securities Identification Procedures* number, more commonly known as a CUSIP number—a universally known identification number given to virtually all municipal bonds.
10. *Dated date* (*Issue date*)—date on which the bonds begin accruing interest.
11. *Frequency of interest payments*—number of times interest is paid; the vast majority of municipal bonds pay interest semiannually, for example,

every six months, on cycles starting with the month the bonds are maturing.

12. *Method of calculating interest*—how interest is calculated; most municipal bonds are calculated on a 30-day month, 360-day year.

13. *Next call date and call price if applicable*—if bonds are prerefunded, the term prerefunded is normally substituted for the term call (see Key 22).

14. *Bond rating of the security*—rating as published by Moody's and/or Standard & Poor's.

15. *Payment and delivery instructions*—indication to mail check and hold in safekeeping/custody, for example.

16. *Principal amount*—amount the investor must pay for the bond, excluding the accrued interest. (par value × price / 100); for example, 100,000 × 102 / 100 = $102,000.

17. *Accrued interest*—the amount of interest accrued since the previous payment date or issue date, up until the settlement date. This amount is normally paid by the new purchaser of the security to the prior holder to compensate the previous holder for interest earned since receiving the last payment.

18. *Net amount*—the total sum of the principal amount and the accrued interest. It is the total amount owed to the dealer if bonds are purchased, and the total amount to be received from the dealer if the bonds are sold.

19. *Name and address of the customer.*

20. *Acting as agent*—situation in which, if the dealer is acting in the capacity of agent (securities were never owned by the dealer firm, but purchased by the dealer on behalf of the customer), it will be duly noted on the confirm. In addition, the profit realized by the agent should be disclosed as well.

17

FORMS OF BOND ISSUANCE

Municipal bonds have, over the years, been issued in various forms. Today the vast majority of bonds are book entry—a data entry on a computer—and, to a much lesser extent, registered. The following is a discussion of the ways in which bonds are issued to the investing public.

Book-entry bonds. With the book-entry procedure, by far the most popular method of issuing municipal bonds, they are not issued in physical form, on pieces of paper, but are solely a data entry on a computer system. This is identical to the way Treasury securities are issued. As a result, customers cannot have their bonds sent to their homes, but instead must rely on the custody statements issued by brokerage houses and banks. These statements are normally issued monthly and are evidence of the securities' ownership. To many old-time investors, not being able to have their bonds in the safe deposit box may prove disturbing. But virtually all municipal bonds will eventually be issued in book-entry form.

Two commonly asked questions regarding book-entry securities are:

1. *If the brokerage house or bank goes bankrupt, what happens to my bonds?*

   This is a concern that should be carefully considered. While the probability of a material loss is extremely rare, certain relevant questions must be asked of the broker. Key 52 deals with this question in greater depth.

2. *If I want to stop doing business with the broker, or want to sell my bonds at a different dealer, can the bonds be easily moved?*

Having bonds held in book-entry form does *not* preclude the investor from transferring the book-entry securities between dealers. The investor must simply inform the broker in writing that he/she wishes to transfer these bonds to another broker. No reason needs to be given.

Registered bonds. These are issued in physical form; the bonds are printed on paper. The investor's name and address appear on the bond and are filed with the bond's paying agent, the bank that makes the interest and principal payments to the holders of the bonds, so that interest is mailed to the customer along with the principal repayment when the bond matures. If the bond is called by the issuer prior to maturity, the investor will likewise be notified by the paying agent. Registered bonds are issued much less often than book-entry bonds. For investors averse to purchasing book-entry securities, registered bonds may be the only game in town, offering a limited universe of bonds from which to choose.

Bearer bonds (coupon bonds). These are securities that do not contain information regarding the purchaser's name or address; whoever is in possession of the bond is deemed to be the owner. Unlike registered bonds, interest and principal checks *are not mailed* to the bondholder. Instead, the bondholder must clip the coupons attached to the bond and submit them to the paying agent bank for payment. While no longer issued in the primary market, decreasing amounts of bearer bonds may be found in the resale, or secondary, market. Some investors who like the anonymous nature of bearer bonds actively seek out these bonds and may often pay a premium price for these rare securities; however, this perceived benefit may be offset by two disadvantages:

1. If lost or misplaced, replacing these bonds may be difficult and/or costly.
2. Because no information about the bondholder is on record with a paying agent, the investor will not be notified about the securities being called; therefore, the investor must constantly monitor newspapers and other information sources.

18

COSTS OF BUYING BONDS

There is normally no commission charge associated with the purchase of municipal bonds. Most dealers are compensated through the bid-ask spread: buying a bond at a lower price and subsequently selling at a higher price, thereby earning the difference. Often—hopefully not too often—dealers may, in fact, sell their bonds at a loss. This may occur following a period of rising interest rates that, as discussed previously, erodes the value of bonds held in the dealer's inventory. While the bonds are sold to investors at a loss, this loss may be less severe than if the dealer was forced to sell the bonds to other dealers—back to the street—thereby minimizing the loss to the firm.

The sale of municipal bonds, can be categorized as follows:

Riskless principal involves a relatively riskless transaction where the dealer buys bonds at the direction of a specific customer and then sells the bonds to this customer at a markup from the price at which the dealer bought the bonds. This markup can vary widely depending on the bond's maturity and quality, size of the block of bonds, and the profit that the dealer may be looking to realize. Remember, *there is not one uniform price for a municipal bond*. Dealers often attempt to mark up the bond's price as much as they can get away with. On a $25,000 purchase, for example, the dealer can attempt to make anywhere from $50 to more than $1,000. Often, repeat customers with considerable net worth can demand more advantageous pricing. However, it is important for all municipal bond investors to become as knowledgeable as possible, comparing prices among several dealers.

Risk trades involve the sale of municipal bonds from the dealer's inventory. Traders may purchase bonds, hoping that the prices of the securities will appreciate in value. They could then be resold to other dealers or to the firm's customers at a substantial profit. However, realistically, this may or may not materialize and, in fact, dealers may sell bonds at a loss if the bond market turns against them. Therefore, it is moot to speak of a markup in this case, as the dealer is subject to some degree of risk. More important to the investor, than what the dealer is earning on a sale, is whether the bonds being offered are at an attractive price relative to comparable bonds offered by other dealers.

Commission trades are trades that, while not normally industry practice, may contain an additional commission charge tacked on by some smaller brokerage houses to any municipal bond purchase. This charge may be in lieu of, or in addition to, the profit earned from marking up the price of the bonds.

19

MARKETABILITY OF BONDS

The issue of the marketability or salability of municipal bonds arises out of an investor's need to sell his/her bonds prior to its stated maturity date.

When purchasing municipal bonds, an investor should attempt to match the bonds' maturity with an estimated future need. For example, if an individual is planning to buy a house in three years, then a three-year bond should be bought—not a twenty-year bond with the intent to sell it in three years. However, if an unexpected crisis occurs, the investor may be forced to sell the bonds in the after-sale or secondary market. The question then arises: Will the investor be able to sell his/her specific bond, and if so, will the investor be able to sell it at a "fair price" (get a good bid)? There are several factors that will affect the marketability of one's municipal bonds.

Block size. The smaller the size of the block of bonds, the less marketable. A wealthy individual selling a $500,000 block will receive a price that better approximates the bond's "true value" than one selling a block of $10,000. This is the result of a built-in demand for large blocks of bonds by bond traders, corporations, bond funds, and wealthy individuals. These institutional players generally know the true value of a block of bonds, and most often will shy away from those annoying odd lots.

Quality and notoriety of bonds. The higher-quality, well-known names will demand a better bid than esoteric, low-quality issues. For example, an AAA Westchester County general obligation bond will be more salable than an unrated New York City industrial development bond.

Market conditions. Market conditions in the muni-bond market play a vital role in determining the marketability of an investor's bonds. In the U.S. Treasury market, investors can sell their securities under almost any market conditions. However, in the municipal bond market, following negative market news we can see the bid side on municipals—the price at which dealers will buy bonds—fall dramatically, and, in some cases, completely disappear, when bonds cannot be sold at any price. It is recommended that, unless no other remedy exists, muni-bonds should not be sold into a "panic bid." It is normally better to wait until market conditions stabilize prior to selling.

The broker. Some municipal bond dealers make a living buying customers' bonds at artificially low prices, substantially below their true market value. Investors are advised to shop around, soliciting bids from several dealers before selling.

Although there may be many compelling reasons touted by your broker for swapping your bonds (see Key 51), it is strongly recommended that the small investor use a buy-and-hold policy due to the relative inefficiency of the municipal bond market. A caveat; remember, if forced to sell prior to maturity, shop around!

20

MUNICIPAL BOND MUTUAL FUNDS

Municipal bond funds are for investors seeking tax-free income, but not interested in becoming municipal bond experts who devote time to learn and invest in specific tax-free bonds. It's also ideal for those investors who do not have sufficient funds to meet the minimum requirements of investing in single bonds, $5,000 being the smallest denomination in which bonds are issued today. Furthermore, it is imperative that investors diversify by not putting all their eggs in one basket. An investor with total investment funds of $10,000, for example, can only buy bonds of two issuers. This is not sufficient diversification!

What Is a Municipal Bond Mutual Fund? A municipal bond mutual fund is a pool of short-, intermediate-, or long-term municipal bonds, or a combination of all three, purchased by a manager on behalf of investors. When investors buy shares in a municipal bond fund, they are, in effect, buying a cross-section of the overall portfolio— a small slice of each bond in the fund. The interest on the municipal bonds that comprise the portfolio flows through tax free to the purchasers of the fund. The purchaser's shares are redeemable on demand at their current value or, more precisely, at the shares' *net asset value,* derived by dividing the fund's total worth by the number of shares outstanding.

The net asset value of a bond fund will thus rise or fall in tandem with the price of the bonds that comprise the fund. If, on the whole, the bonds in the portfolio rise in value since their purchase date, the investor will enjoy a gain. Conversely, if the value of the underlying bonds fall in value, the investor will realize a loss. Thus, while a mutual bond fund is liquid in the sense of being able to convert shares into cash on demand, it must be stressed that this conversion may be done at a gain or loss. Unlike Unit Investment Trusts (UITs) (see Key 21), mutual fund managers *trade the underlying portfolio,* buying and selling bonds, and booking the gain or loss, and simultaneously passing the *realized* gain or loss along to shareholders. By employing this strategy, the fund's manager is attempting to generate tax-free income, as well as looking to preserve capital, that is avoid taking capital losses on the bond portfolio. This is accomplished by anticipating moves in interest rates, and constantly monitoring credit quality of the underlying issues. It is often the case however, that these professional money managers act after the fact, selling when the bond prices have already fallen. As a general rule, municipal bond mutual funds tend to rise in value during periods of falling rates and rising bond prices, and fall in value during periods of rising rates and falling bond prices because even the best fund managers have difficulty predicting market movements. This can be compared to a stock market money manager who normally finds it easier to pick "good" stocks when the stock market, as a whole, is rising. Moreover, when bond prices are moving downward precipitously, the only safe haven is *cash.* As a rule, mutual fund managers have a tough time committing the majority of the fund's assets to cash, or cash equivalents, as this strategy makes it difficult for money managers to justify their existence. Let's face it—who needs to pay a professional money manager to keep one's cash in the bank!

Types of Municipal Bond Mutual Funds.

Load vs. no-load. A load is nothing more than a sales charge or commission paid to the sellers of various mutual funds. A load, or sales commission, can vary from one quarter of 1 percent to 8.5 percent, the maximum allowed by the NASD, depending on the particular fund and on the dollar amount purchased. A reduction in the normal sales charge is achieved by the fund's offering *breakpoints* (when a specified dollar amount is purchased, the sales charge drops). For example, a breakpoint over $100,000 may drop the sales charge from 4 percent to 2 percent, and over $500,000 to 1 percent. A load can be paid at the time of purchase, as an addition to the price paid per share (front load), or at the time of redemption (back-end load). In effect, the front load reduces the amount of money actually being invested. In many cases, the back-end load is reduced annually. Thus, the longer the fund is held by the investor, the lower the sales charge at redemption time.

A no-load fund, as the name suggests, is a mutual bond fund that charges no front or back-end load. These funds are typically purchased directly from the fund managers, eliminating the need to pay mutual fund salespeople. All things being equal, paying no sales charge is preferable over paying one; therefore, the investor must decide whether a load fund is so outstanding—has exhibited superior returns over time—that it justifies paying an added charge.

Short-, intermediate-, or long-term bond funds. Municipal bond mutual funds can be classified according to the maturity structure or *average life* (average maturity) of the bonds that comprise the fund. As a general rule, the longer the average life of the bond fund, the greater the income and expected return, but the greater the volatility as well. The shorter the average life, the lower the income or expected return, but the greater the price stability. In an environment of rising bond prices (falling interest rates), investors in long-term bond funds will enjoy the greatest gains. Conversely, in a period of falling bond prices (rising interest rates), investors in long-term bond funds bear the largest losses. There can be no better example of this than in 1994 when many of these long-term bond fund buyers, spoiled by the previous years of falling rates and the subsequent appreciation in the price of bonds, learned a very expensive lesson. The value of municipal bond funds declined precipitously, wiping out a good deal of wealth in the process. A $100,000 investment in a long-term bond fund in early 1994, for example, could have fallen in value to $75,000 by year end! Those investors desiring as little market risk as possible should seek out funds with the shortest average lives. For those wishing to have no fluctuation in price, a tax-exempt money market mutual fund is the way to go.

Tax-exempt money market mutual funds. A tax-exempt money market mutual fund can be viewed as a tax-free checking or savings account. The fund is managed, but not guaranteed, to maintain a $1.00 per share net asset value. By purchasing relatively short maturities of municipal notes (Key 27), variable-rate demand bonds (Key 29), etc., the fund manager, in effect, eliminates the price fluctuations associated with normal bond funds. According to SEC rules, investments in money market accounts cannot have maturities that exceed 13 months, or a portfolio average life of more than 90 days. While returns on tax-exempt money market funds are relatively low, as compared to longer-term bond funds, they are the only appropriate fund investments for those seeking a liquid, short-term alternative to conventional taxable checking and money market accounts.

Investing in a Municipal Bond Fund. When purchasing municipal bond funds investors should:

1. view municipal bond funds as long-term investments;
2. read the prospectus thoroughly;
3. note the fund's *expense ratio*. This ratio reveals, as a percentage of the fund's assets, how much the fund is paying in various expenses, such as administrative costs. All things being equal, the lower the expense ratio, the better. As with loads, it is up to the investor to determine whether the fund's superior results justify an above-average expense ratio;
4. note the different average lives of particular funds; and
5. consider dollar cost averaging. Dollar cost averaging involves buying a steady sum of a particular fund over a certain period of time, thus averaging out the overall price for shares of the fund. Dollar cost averaging normally results in a lower average cost per share.

21

UNIT INVESTMENT TRUST (UIT)

A municipal unit investment trust (UIT) in many ways is similar to a municipal bond fund (see Key 20). Investors, once again, are able to earn tax-exempt interest income without the need to learn about and purchase individual bonds. Through an investment of as little as $1,000—individual bonds are normally issued with minimum denominations of $5,000—the investor receives the benefit of instant diversification, spreading out the risk among the many bonds in the portfolio. However, these benefits never come cheap, since there is normally a sales charge or load, usually 4 to 5 percent of the amount invested.

Like a municipal bond fund manager, a UIT sponsor purchases various (normally long-term) municipal bonds, creating a diversified municipal bond portfolio. Shares, or, in UIT terminology, units, are sold to investors who, in effect, are buying a cross-section—a slice of each bond—of the underlying portfolio. The primary difference between a UIT and a mutual bond fund is that UITs are *not managed*. Once the trust is *closed*, in which all shares in the UIT are sold and the trust is in effect, "sold out," the trading (buying or selling of any bonds) ceases. Bonds are thus purchased by the sponsor with the intent of holding them to maturity or until they are called, at the discretion of the issuer. When this occurs, funds are distributed to shareholders rather than reinvested in new bonds. Since there is no proactive management associated with unit investment trusts, once the trust is closed, expenses tend to be minimal, considerably less than with bond mutual funds.

While the UIT managers do not trade the portfolio—continually buying, then reselling bonds, booking gains and losses, and then passing them along to shareholders—the value of the UIT shares, or units, nonetheless fluctuate with the value of the underlying bond portfolio. Evaluators continually judge the worth of the trust's underlying bonds in order to determine the current unit price, the value of trust divided by number of units. Investors in need of their principal can redeem the shares at the determined price—normally free of any additional charge—through the trustee who provides an aftersale market for these shares. While the price of the units fluctuates throughout the life of the trust, the investor, by patiently waiting until the bonds in the trust mature, can be assured—assuming no bankruptcies—of receiving back the initial investment.

Investors with significant investment capital and a good deal of knowledge about municipal bonds can bypass the UIT in favor of creating their own bond portfolios. If the UIT is chosen as the appropriate investment vehicle, the investor is urged to purchase either an insured trust or one containing high-quality bonds. Too often, UITs purchase low-quality bonds to boost their advertised yields.

22

PREREFUNDED BONDS (TAX-FREE TREASURIES)

Prerefunded bonds (preres) are one of the best-kept secrets among the financial community. They represent a great bargain for those investors looking for a gilt-edged security coupled with tax-free income. Simply put, prerefunded bonds are municipal bonds that are no longer backed by the issuer but are instead backed by U.S. government securities. In addition, these bonds no longer come due on the stated maturity date but instead mature on a prior call date (see Key 23). Therefore, the investor need not be concerned with the creditworthiness of the issuer or the stated (original) maturity date of the bonds. Rather, the investor should concentrate on the quality of the securities backing the bonds, the integrity of the bonds' financial and legal structure, and whether the call date (new maturity date), fits into the desired maturity structure of his/her portfolio.

The creation of a prerefunded bond is a complex financial procedure that is often a great mystery to even many sophisticated investors; therefore, a comprehensive discussion of the structuring, and pitfalls of prerefunded bonds are required at this time.

Similar to a homeowner who refinances his/her old high-interest rate mortgage in favor of a current lower rate mortgage, preres are created by the issuer who refinances its older higher coupon rate bonds by issuing new bonds at lower prevailing interest rates. It is only these older bonds that concerned us, since these are the bonds that become the prerefunded bonds. Thus preres cannot be found in the new issue market since they are by definition old, or secondary market, bonds that are transformed into these government-backed securities. The process of creating prerefunded bonds is as follows:

- Taking advantage of a lower interest rate environment, a municipality issues new bonds at the lower prevailing rates.
- With the proceeds of the new issue, it buys zero coupon treasuries (see Key 3), which ultimately back the old bonds.
- In addition, the issuer mandates that these old bonds will no longer come due on the stated maturity date but instead will fall due on the first call date available to the issuer. Thus, this call date becomes the old bonds' new maturity date. In the event the issuer is precluded from calling the bonds at any time prior to the original maturity, it may nonetheless back the old bonds with Treasuries until the final maturity date. The bonds are then called *escrowed to maturity* (ETM), rather than prerefunded.

The following is an example of the creation of a specific prerefunded bond.

Old bond (prior to prerefunding)
Issuer: New York City
Issue date: July 1, 1987
Coupon rate: 8.00 percent
Maturity date: July 1, 2007
Call date: July 1, 1997 @ 102

In 1991 the issuer refinanced these old bonds through the following procedure:

1. New York City mandated that the above-mentioned bonds would unequivocally be called on July 1, 1997, at a premium of 2 percent (102).
2. New York City issued "new bonds" at 6 percent, receiving proceeds (dollars) from investors purchasing the new bonds. Note that this rate is significantly lower than the old bonds coupon rate of 8 percent.

3. With the proceeds of the new issue, zero coupon Treasury bonds were purchased by a third party trustee in sufficient amounts to repay the interest and principal on the old bonds. The maturities on the zero coupon Treasuries exactly matched the interest payment schedule as well as the repayment amounts on the bonds' call date (the new maturity date).

Thus, the old New York City bonds were transformed from a marginal investment grade bond maturing in 2007 to a bond now backed by U.S. government securities maturing in 1997 at 2 percent premium over face value.

The old New York City bonds can now be traded in the aftersale market as a relatively homogeneous Treasury-backed security. An investor can thus call the municipal bond dealer and ask for offerings on prerefunded bonds maturing in various years. Since the supply of prerefunded bonds is a function of what other market participants wish to sell (no new issue market), it may be difficult to obtain a prere maturing on a specific date.

Pitfalls of Prerefunded Bonds. Preres must be backed by 100 percent direct U.S. Treasuries or other securities that are acceptable to the investor. In addition, their financial and legal structure must be ironclad. One way to effectively mitigate these risks is to purchase only those prerefunded bonds that have been reviewed by the rating agencies and consequently rerated AAA, attesting to the bonds' financial integrity and quality of those securities backing the bonds. For example, for Moody's to rerate an issue Aaa, the bonds must be escrowed (backed) by direct U.S. Treasuries, or by securities that are unconditionally backed by the U.S. Treasury.

Due to the normally high coupon rate and the resulting substantial premium paid when purchasing prerefunded bonds, it is of the utmost importance to make sure that the bonds have no calls of any sort, such as a sinking fund (see Key 50) prior to the stated call date. An unexpected early call may substantially reduce the stated YTM or, even worse, result in a financial loss. Have your bond broker confirm this at the time of sale, and insist that this fact is stated in written form, if possible.

23

CALLABLE BONDS

A call feature allows the issuer to redeem a bond on a given date, or dates, prior to maturity, at a specific price. Like a homeowner refinancing a mortgage to exploit a lower interest rate environment, issuers normally call in (redeem) bonds prior to their stated maturity date to refinance at more attractive interest rates.

Bonds can be called at various intervals prior to maturity. General obligation bonds, for example, usually have ten-year call protection, meaning that from the date of issuance the issuer cannot call the bonds for at least ten years.

The following is an example of a General Obligation (G-O) bond.

General Obligation Bond (G-O)
Issuer: New York State
Issue date: 8/01/95
Coupon rate: 7.00 percent
Maturity date: 8/01/15
Call date: 8/01/05 @ 102
Declining to: 100 (par) 8/01/07

1. Bonds cannot be called until the year 2005, a ten-year call protection from the issue date.
2. If the bonds are, in fact, called in 2005, the investor will receive a call premium of 102 (2 percent above par).
3. Following 8/01/05, the bonds can continually be called. A common bond structure allows the bond to be called every six months following the first call date at a half of 1 percent lower premium. For example:

2/01/06 @ 101.5
8/01/06 @ 101
2/01/07 @ 100.5
8/01/07 and
later @ 100

Thus, we see that if called on or after 2/01/07, the investor is not compensated with any premium whatsoever.

The call scenario discussed above is the most popular and the best understood by most investors. This type of call is often referred to as a stated call, because it is stated clearly in the official statement (see Key 55) and printed on the customer confirmation. If exercised by the issuer, the entire maturity must be called, not just a prorated portion. When selling callable bonds, dealers must take into consideration these calls in determining the bond's price.

In addition to stated calls, there are other less publicized calls associated primarily with housing, student loan, and health care bonds, with which the investor should become familiar. They are generally referred to as *extraordinary calls,* and include:

- *Unexpended proceeds calls.* These calls allow the issuer to redeem bonds, usually at par, from moneys not spent following the construction of a project. They often result in only a portion of an investor's bonds being called.
- *Condemnation calls.* Calls in which, in the event a project is condemned, the issuer has a right to redeem bonds, normally at par.
- *Prepayment calls.* These calls allow the issuer to redeem bonds prior to maturity from prepayments of mortgages. Once again, it should be noted that these calls often result in only a prorated portion of bonds being called.
- *Student loan repayment calls.* As the name suggests, these calls are involved solely with student loan bonds. They deal with the early redemption of bonds normally at par, from the early repayment of student loans.

Although stated calls are disclosed to the customer, as printed on the confirmation, and are considered when determining the price paid for a bond, extraordinary calls are not. Often, brokers ignore the whole concept when they are attempting to sell bonds to investors. When considering the purchase of any housing bond, health care bond, or student loan bond, the investor should ascertain whether any of these extraordinary calls are in effect. While any unexpected call can lead to a return of one's funds at an undesirable time, investors should be extremely cognizant of these calls when purchasing premium bonds.

An unexpected call can significantly reduce a premium bond's return. Additionally, in some cases, it may also cause the purchaser to incur a substantial financial loss.

24

ZERO COUPON (CAPITAL APPRECIATION) BONDS

As the name suggests, zero coupon bonds do not pay the investor a tidy sum each year. Rather, the investor purchases the bonds at a discount to (price less than) face value and receives only one single (bullet) payment at maturity when the bonds are redeemed for the face value amount. The difference between the amount paid at the initial purchase and the amount received at maturity is normally considered tax-exempt interest.

Who Should Own Zero Coupon Bonds?

1. Investors who have little or no need for current income, and are concerned instead with having their funds grow without the burden of reinvesting interest income.
2. Parents looking to finance a child's college education often find municipal zero coupons an invaluable investment vehicle. Due to the magic of compound interest, a paltry sum invested today can grow to a significant payment toward the ever-increasing cost of a college education. Many municipal issuers now offer college saver bonds that are nothing more than your run-of-the-mill zero coupon bonds, coupled with a Madison Avenue touch.
3. Zero coupon municipal bonds may be an ideal investment for those wishing to accumulate money toward retirement or toward other long-term

financial goals, such as accumulating sufficient funds to buy that dream house. As in the case of parents financing their children's college education, funds likewise compound without the need to reinvest interest.

4. Sophisticated investors seeking maximum volatility should consider zero coupons as a vehicle to exploit these market movements. Zeros enable investors to leverage their investments. With an initial investment of $75,000, for example, the investor may be able to purchase a block of bonds with a face value of $250,000, thereby increasing his/her gain in an up market, while losing more in a down market. In technical terms, since zeros pay no interest until maturity, their duration—a weighted average measure taking into account interest payments, quantifying how quickly an investor gets his/her money back—is longer than that of a normal, or full coupon bond that generates interest every six months. By definition, the longer a bond's duration, the more volatility it will display, rising in price faster than a conventional bond in a bull market, where there are rising bond prices, and falling more rapidly in a bear market, where there are falling bond prices.

Pitfalls of Zero Coupon Bonds.

1. Those seeking income now should avoid capital appreciation bonds at all costs. Investors seeking to maximize current income should stick to conventional municipal bonds that normally pay interest twice a year.

2. Zero coupon bonds are considered less marketable than normal full coupon interest-bearing bonds, especially when dealing with odd lots (blocks of $25,000 or less); therefore, it is of the utmost importance to avoid, if possible, having to sell your zero coupon bonds in the resale, or secondary market. However, for high net worth individuals with large trading blocks—$250,000 or more—the zero coupon resale market may prove a much friendlier place.

3. While it is widely understood that the difference between the purchase price of a municipal zero coupon and its redemption price is considered tax-free interest, little is known about a technicality within our tax law that may subject a portion of the income on a zero coupon purchased in the secondary market to capital gains taxes. While highly complex, by simply following this rule, the investor will be helped to avoid any IRS problems:

- Ask your broker for the original yield that the bonds were offered at the time of their initial offering in the primary market; assume a YTM = 7 percent.
- If the YTM that you receive on the zero purchased in the aftersale market is less than the original yield of 7 percent, there is no capital gain involved; it would be similar to buying a conventional interest-bearing bond at a premium.
- If the YTM you receive on the zero purchased in the aftersale market is greater than the original yield of 7 percent, a capital gain is indeed involved, and the true after-tax yield must be calculated. It would be similar to buying a conventional interest-bearing bond at a discount. The bond broker can calculate the true after-capital gain YTM (see Key 8).

Unique Types of Zero Coupon Bonds.

1. *Zero coupon prerefunded bonds.* These bonds retain the same properties as conventional prerefunded bonds (see Key 22), except they carry no coupon and thus pay no current income. Whereas, interest-bearing preres are normally prerefunded (called at) a premium, such as 102 or 102 percent, zero coupon preres are generally prerefunded at less than 100 percent of the bond's face value, such as 85 or 85 percent. The esoteric nature of this instrument precludes many unsophisticated investors from even considering their purchase. As

a result, the discerning investor may be rewarded with additional yield to compensate for the complexity of this vehicle.

2. *Convertible zeros.* These are issued as zero coupon bonds but, at some point, prior to maturity, convert to an interest-bearing security; for example, $100,000 zero coupon bonds maturing July 1, 2001, convertible July 1, 1998, to a 10 percent coupon, with a 6 percent yield to maturity (YTM). The broker, using a high-powered bond brain (calculator) will calculate the price that will generate this quoted return. Purchasing this type of instrument would be conducive for an investor needing no additional income for a number of years, but at some point in the future, such as upon retirement, needing an increase in income. If the investor can match that date with the conversion date, a well-suited investment vehicle is created. As with other relatively complex securities, additional returns may be offered to compensate for its arcane nature.

3. *Strips.* These bonds are very similar to original issue zero coupon municipal bonds, except that they are created by bond dealers through the breaking up of traditional bonds. This entails separating the coupons from the bonds and selling each coupon as a stand-alone security. Like original issue zero coupon bonds, strips are sold at a discount to face value, and pay no periodic interest payments. While difficult to differentiate between the two, strips may possess odd maturity values, such as 102, for example, and may not be rated by Moody's or Standard & Poor's.

25

HIGH-YIELD MUNICIPAL BONDS (JUNK BONDS)

While high-yield municipals may offer the sophisticated municipal bond investor the potential for above-average returns, they nonetheless represent a potential disaster for the unsuspecting neophyte investor. High-yield municipal bonds, at best, have speculative elements that threaten the ultimate repayment of the bonds and, at worst, may actually be in default (trading flat, paying no interest) with a small chance of ever becoming a secure investment.

While high, possibly double-digit returns quoted by a broker may seem tempting, the investor must be able to determine whether this expected return—remember, the yield to maturity assumes that the bonds are repaid in full—adequately compensates for the possibility of losing the principal. Furthermore, high-yield municipals are illiquid, at times with a small or no resale market to speak of. Thus, the purchaser may end up holding the bonds for a long period of time.

Various firms specialize in municipal junk bonds and devote numerous hours analyzing quite complex situations. Identifying a turnaround situation may result in the reaping of extraordinary returns. Sophisticated investors—those who do a plethora of research and who fully understand the risks associated with the specific bond—may, in the long run, be rewarded by extremely high returns as well.

Beginner investors should avoid junk bonds at all costs; only municipal bonds of investment grade (see Key 46) should be considered for purchase. For all of those sophisticated investors willing to risk their principal and participate in the high-yield municipal market, the following is advised:

1. Only financially astute investors with a financial background should play in the junk bond market.
2. Dedicate lots of time and effort researching the bonds.
3. Have the utmost confidence in your broker's knowledge and integrity.
4. *Diversify!* Don't put all your eggs in one basket, *especially one with a large hole in it.*
5. Have access to numerous research reports and other information sources relating to the high-yield bond in question.
6. Invest only sums that you can afford to lose and that will not be needed in the near future.
7. Consider investing in junk bonds through a municipal high-yield bond fund that provides instant diversification and professional management.
8. *Most of all, be careful!*

26

PUT BONDS

A put allows the investor to relinquish his/her bonds to the issuer, or a third party, and receive the principal some time prior to the bond's maturity. In effect, the put date can be viewed as the bond's real maturity date if the investor so wishes. Depending on a bond's structure, a put can be exercised at any number of specified time intervals. Common put periods include daily, weekly, semiannually, and annually, as well as three- and five-year intervals.

EXAMPLE:
Bond's Purchase Date: July 1, 1995
Maryland Community Development Administration
  (CDA)
6.00 percent coupon maturing July 7, 2008
Putable: July 1, 2000

While the stated maturity date is 13 years from the date of purchase, the relevant maturity date is, in fact, the put date, which allows the investor to tender his/her bonds to the Maryland CDA in five years.

Associated with many financial structures, put bonds can be of two basic types: optional put and mandatory put.

Optional put. With an optional put the investor must initiate the put process; otherwise the bonds are considered retained. At some period prior to the actual stated put date—a common window period is 15 to 30 days prior to the put—the investor must notify the broker whether he/she wishes to tender his/her bond. If the investor decides to tender the bond, the bond will then be paid off on the put date. If retained, the investor will hold the bond either to maturity or to the next put date, when the identical process is then repeated. Often, when deciding whether to tender the bond during the window period, the investor is given incomplete information regarding the new coupon rate for the next period. In other words, a range may be given notifying the investor that the new reset rate is between 4 percent and 4½ percent. This fact, coupled with the chance of forgetting to notify the broker on time, may lead some investors to treat the initial put date as the maturity date, notifying the broker at the time of the initial bond purchase that he/she wishes to have the bonds put unless otherwise notified. This places the onus on the brokerage firm to remember to put the bonds.

Mandatory put. A mandatory put for all intents and purposes can be treated by the investor as identical to a bond's maturity. The investor need not be proactive because the bonds will automatically be redeemed by the issuer on the put date.

Due to changes in the tax law (Tax Reform Act of 1986), the issuance and secondary market trading of put bonds has declined significantly. However, the concept of putting, or tendering one's bonds prior to maturity, is an invaluable concept in understanding the workings of the short-term municipal market.

27

MUNICIPAL NOTES

Municipal notes are short-term obligations issued by municipalities to meet cash flow borrowing needs. Not to be confused with Treasury notes (see Key 3), municipal notes normally mature in a year or less and pay interest at maturity rather than semiannually like bonds. In analyzing the creditworthiness of a municipality's note issue, great emphasis is placed on cash flow because of the short-term nature of the security.

The basic questions that must be answered, prior to investing in notes are: Will there be enough cash on hand when the notes come due, and/or can the notes be successfully rolled over?

The most common type of municipal notes are tax anticipation notes (TANs), revenue anticipation notes (RANs), tax and revenue anticipation notes (TRANs), and bond anticipation notes (BANs).

1. *Tax anticipation notes* are issued in anticipation of future tax collections.
2. *Revenue anticipation notes* are issued in anticipation of some form of revenue other than taxes, such as state aid. For example, school districts are major issuers of RANs, because in many instances, a significant portion of their budget consists of state aid.
3. *Tax and revenue anticipation notes,* as the name suggests, are issued in anticipation of a combination of both taxes and other sources of revenue, such as state aid.
4. *Bond anticipation notes* are issued in anticipation of an inevitable longer-term bond issuance. A BAN can be compared to a homeowner obtaining a bridge loan prior to taking out a 15- or 30-year mortgage. However, in actuality, BANs may very often be

rolled over many times before the issuer finally floats a bond issue; therefore, access to the capital markets is the primary requisite for repayment.

All things being equal, TANs , RANs, and TRANs are considered more creditworthy than BANs, since the payment of the former three types of notes is not contingent upon access to financial markets. Even if the municipality is able to have access to the market, rolling over an issue during a period of high short-term interest rates may very well prove to be a financial strain for the issuer. Nonetheless, this is a fine distinction, because ultimately BANs, like the other listed short-term obligations, are backed by the full faith and credit of the municipality.

Cash Flow Notes or Seasonal Borrowing Notes. TANs, RANs, and TRANs are considered cash flow notes or seasonal borrowing notes since their purpose is to allow municipalities to meet various liquidity crunches throughout the fiscal year. For example, in the case of a school district in need of dollars to purchase books and other supplies in the summer, prior to the beginning of the school year, and with the collection of taxes still months away, a TAN issue may be just what the doctor ordered.

It is the proceeds of the note issue that makes it possible to purchase all the required books and supplies. Even with the knowledge that the notes will be repaid with the annual collection of school taxes, it is also imperative to consider the following:

1. What is the projected cash flow for the upcoming period?
2. Concerning the history of tax collections, is the municipality collecting the taxes due in a sufficient amount and on a timely basis?
3. Is a disproportionate amount of revenue coming from one source, such as state aid or one major industrial taxpayer?
4. Is the municipality relying too heavily on short-term debt?

When analyzing note issues, both Moody's and Standard & Poor's often designate special short-term ratings, taking into account some of the questions posed above. These ratings, MIG 1 and SP1+, for example, as discussed in Key 46, are also assigned in addition to the municipality's underlying long-term rating. Occasionally, it is quite possible for an issuer with a weak underlying rating to receive the top short-term rating. For example, New York City, with a marginal underlying rating of Baa1, nonetheless most often receives a MIG1 short-term rating on its note issues. What Moody's is, in effect, saying, is that "while many problems may persist that could threaten the city's long-term viability, for the time being there is enough money around to pay off short-term noteholders."

28

MUNICIPAL AUCTION PREFERRED STOCK

Municipal auction preferred stock (MAPS), utilized primarily by corporations, has recently gained popularity among high net worth individuals. These investors are seeking an alternative to conventional short-term tax-exempt investment vehicles, such as municipal notes, lower floaters, and tax-exempt money market mutual funds. While municipal auction preferred stock offers the sophisticated investor protection of principal, high relative after-tax returns, and a good degree of liquidity, it is nonetheless an extremely complex financial instrument, despite the simplistic way it is represented by some brokers.

At first glance, the unsuspecting investor may understand MAPS to be just another tax-free bond, maturing in 7 or 28 days, normally rated AAA, paying a yield to maturity quite competitive with other short-term instruments. While the facts stated are essentially true, MAPS are anything but a run-of-the-mill tax-free bond. First, as the name suggests, MAPS are not bonds at all, but shares of *preferred stock* of a municipal bond fund (see Key 20). The underlying fund is comprised of a diversified portfolio of investment grade tax-exempt securities. Since bonds held in this fund are exclusively municipals, the dividends paid to shareholders pass through tax free. Shareholders of these funds include both preferred and common. Common shares trade on the New York and American stock exchanges, about which an in-depth discussion is not pertinent at this time. Preferred shareholders are always considered senior to common shareholders in the event of a default, and thus have the initial claim on the fund's assets. According to the 1940 Investment Act, these funds must maintain a minimum of 200 percent asset coverage for these preferred shares. Simply stated, for every $1.00 of municipal auction preferred, there must be at least $2.00 worth of bonds in the portfolio, which the preferred shareholder (MAPS holder) can have claim to. In the event the coverage falls below 200 percent, due to a decline in the value of the bonds comprising the portfolio, for example, the fund must immediately redeem shares to bring the fund back into compliance with the law. Based on this financial structure, the rating agencies normally assign an AAA rating to MAPS issues.

MAPS is a perpetual instrument, that is, one with no ending maturity date, whose yield resets at various intervals, such as 7 days or 28 days, through a *Dutch auction* (as explained below). This auction is also the means by which investors can get back their funds, since these securities have no real maturity date.

Dutch Auction. A Dutch auction differs from a conventional auction in that only one *clearing rate*—the rate at which all sellers sell at par, and all buyers purchase the preferred stock at par, bringing supply and demand into "equilibrium"—is set. All participants who win shares in the auction thus receive the *identical rate.*

On the auction date, the investor advises his broker to either:

- *sell*—no matter what the new interest rate is reset at, the investor wants his/her funds now!
- *hold*—no matter what the new interest rate is reset at, the investor wants to keep his/her securities until at least the next auction.
- *bid*—the investor can specify the minimum rate at which he/she wants to keep the shares. If the reset rate exceeds, or equals, the "bid," the bidder will buy the MAPS, hold it until the next auction, and receive whatever rate is set.

Remember, in a Dutch auction, all investors who retain their shares will receive the identical interest rate, even if the investor's bid is below the equilibrium rate set. For example, an investor with a bid of 4.00 percent for

$1,000,000 of MAPS in an auction where the clearing rate is 4.25 percent, would receive a rate of 4.25 percent. In other financial auctions, such as the U.S. Treasury, investors receive whatever they bid, whether or not other investors get higher returns.

Risks of MAPS. Due to the generally high quality of the underlying bond portfolio, coupled with the broad coverage (minimum 200 percent) mandated by law, the investor's credit risk is negligible, and the securities are thus rated AAA. However, it is important to note that this rating has nothing to do with the stock's liquidity risk—the ability of the investor to tender or sell the securities at the auction and receive funds on time. The MAPS investor's mechanism for receiving the funds is the Dutch auction. Therefore, the primary risk of these securities is that of a failed auction, where no other investor is willing to buy the investor's shares. This risk is mitigated by two factors:

1. In the event of a failed auction, the rate on the MAPS would be automatically set at an extremely high yield. At this inflated return, the investor could hopefully sell the bonds in the aftersale market, not through the Dutch auction mechanism, but directly to other investors, with a dealer firm acting as an intermediary, without incurring a market loss.
2. The Dutch auction process has served these securities well, as no municipal auction has ever failed since the market's inception in 1988.

Municipal Auction Preferred Stock Issuers. The best-known and respected issuers include Nuveen, Intercapital, Blackrock, Van Kampen Merrit, Muniyield, Munivest, and Munienhanced. The municipal auction rate preferred stock issued by these firms is typically rated AAA by Standard & Poor's and Aaa by Moody's.

29

VARIABLE-RATE DEMAND BONDS (LOWER FLOATERS)

While variable-rate demand bonds, also known as lower floaters, are primarily purchased by money market mutual funds and corporations, wealthy individuals often purchase these securities as an alternative to tax-exempt money market funds and other short-term tax-exempt instruments. Dealers often require a minimum purchase of $500,000 to $1,000,000. This requirement, in effect, precludes the small investor from participating in the lower floater arena.

What Is a Variable-Rate Demand Bond (Lower Floater)? A variable-rate demand bond is a long-term tax-exempt municipal bond—maturities can be as long as 30 years—that is converted by a dealer firm into a short-term security.

These bonds are issued for industrial development and pollution control projects, as well as education, housing, health care, and transportation needs through a quasi-governmental agency, such as an industrial development agency. These types of agencies are normally in existence to promote industrial development in a particular area by allowing a corporate entity to borrow money at favorable tax-exempt interest rates. They do not in any way lend their credit backing to the bonds.

Because the backing on the bonds is derived from the creditworthiness of these often small, corporate issuers (a circumstance that is not readily known by investors), a major bank is brought on board, to guarantee timely repayment of interest and principal. The issue is thus characterized as being backed by a *letter of credit* from a bank. In addition, the same, or a different bank, acts as a *remarketing agent,* whose principal responsibility is to find a buyer for the bonds (remarket the bonds) when the current holder wishes to "put" (relinquish) them. The remarketing agent maintains the ability, at various intervals—daily, or weekly—to adjust, either higher or lower, the coupon rate on the bond to make sure someone buys them.

It is this changing coupon rate, when it is coupled with the ability of an investor to put the bonds at various intervals (such as weekly or upon giving the remarketing agent sufficient notice—five business days, for instance) that converts these long-term bonds into short-term instruments.

The following example helps to illustrate and clarify the concept.

XYZ Widget Company wishes to build a factory in New York City. It applies to the New York City Industrial Development Agency (NYC IDA) for the authorization to issue bonds through the agency at the advantaged tax-exempt interest rates. Meeting the criteria for issuance—the factory will help promote jobs in New York City—the NYC Industrial Development Agency issues the following bonds on behalf of XYZ Widget Company.

Because the creditworthiness of XYZ is not widely known by the investing public, the Bank of the United States (which is a major U.S. bank) is brought in to back the bonds. The Bank of Georgia is called in as well, to remarket the bonds. Investors who wish to relinquish their bonds must notify the Bank of Georgia at least five business days in advance.

- *The Bond:* NYC Industrial Development Agency (for XYZ Widget Company), maturing July 1, 2010.

- *The Backing of the Bond:* Letter of Credit—Bank of the United States, as well as the XYZ Widget Company (not the NYC IDA).

- *Interest Rate:* Variable rate, adjusting weekly (every Wednesday).

- *Remarketing Agent:* Bank of Georgia.

- *Notification Period:* Five business days.

Although the actual maturity of the bond is in the year 2010, the investor, in fact, is purchasing a weekly bond. While the stated issuer is the NYC IDA, the real backing on the bonds is obtained from the letter of credit bank, and to a somewhat lesser degree from the XYZ Widget Company.

Investors are urged to purchase only those variable-rate demand bonds with the letters of credit from major highly rated banks.

30

GENERAL OBLIGATION BONDS

Two major events that impact the way general obligation bonds (G-Os) are both analyzed and viewed by the investing public are New York City's mid-1970s financial collapse and subsequent technical default, and the recent and equally disastrous Orange County, California, bankruptcy. Both of these events tarnished the general obligation pledge, and forced securities firms and individuals to conduct serious research and analysis prior to investing in general obligation bonds. (See Key 53.)

General obligation bonds are backed by a municipality's full faith and credit. Principal and interest are supported by the issuer's ability to levy taxes on real property, sales, and income. Voter approval is normally required for a municipality to issue a G-O bond. While the overwhelming majority of general obligation bonds are backed solely by the broad taxing powers of the municipality, some G-Os have the added security of a designated income stream further securing the bond. These bonds are often referred to as *double-barreled bonds*. Historically, general obligation defaults have been extremely rare. If a municipality experiences a revenue shortfall, it is required either to raise taxes or reduce spending to eliminate the deficit. An inherent threat of banishment from the capital markets, indicating an inability to borrow funds from the public, looms for the issuer who dares to walk away from, or repudiate, its financial obligations.

Analysis of General Obligation Debt. When assessing the creditworthiness of a municipality's general obligation debt, the following areas must be examined:

87

- underlying economic conditions
- financial factors
- debt levels
- political factors

Underlying economic conditions. A municipality's underlying economic base is of critical importance in assessing its creditworthiness. Investors must examine a municipality's population trends, wealth levels, employment growth, real estate valuations, and other demographic factors. A declining population, combined with falling income levels, may prove troublesome for a municipality with little financial cushion.

An in-depth analysis of a municipality's tax base must be performed, concentrating on its magnitude, diversity, and composition. Analysts look for a large, diversified group of taxpayers, since an overreliance on a few major industries and/or companies can spell disaster in the event of a business downturn or industrial exodus. In the official statement/prospectus (see Key 55), one can normally find a breakdown of the ten largest taxpayers. It may be useful to examine this information to ascertain whether the municipality is too reliant on one or several major taxpayers.

Financial factors. It is essential for the investor to ascertain how well the municipality keeps its financial house in order. This can begin with an in-depth analysis of the issuer's *revenue stream,* attempting to answer the following questions.

1. Where is the municipality's revenue coming from?
2. Are revenues derived from one particular source, or are they diversified?
3. Has the municipality's revenue stream been stable, growing, or declining over the past several years (the trend of the revenue stream)?

Analysts prefer to see a diversified, growing revenue stream. It is important to remember that certain types of municipalities customarily have a more varied revenue stream than others. For example, a state's revenue base is made up of property taxes, corporate and individual income taxes, sales taxes, gift and inheritance taxes, federal aid, and so on, whereas a local municipality such as a school district, relies principally on real estate taxes.

Analysts can review the *spending habits of a municipality* in an expenditure analysis to ascertain whether spending is in line with the revenue received. They must determine if this continued pattern of spending will result in a need to increase taxes to make up for any shortfall.

The municipality's *fund balance,* which can be viewed simply as cash in the bank, as well as the trend of the fund balance, must be analyzed. A large, increasing fund balance may be evidence of financial flexibility, assuring enough cash on hand to weather a cyclical downturn and an accompanying liquidity crisis.

Debt levels. The municipality's existing level of debt must be examined in order to ascertain the amount of debt incurred in relation to its size or revenue, the structure of the debt—for instance, is the municipality borrowing on a long- or short-term basis—the repayment schedule of the debt, and whether capacity exists for future borrowing to meet capital needs. The less borrowing a municipality has done in the past, the more it could potentially borrow in the future if the need arises. However, like an individual who has never borrowed and established a credit rating in the past, the lack of *any* borrowing on the part of a municipality may paradoxically lead to the inability for the issuer to borrow in the marketplace.

The maturity structure of the municipality's debt should match the expected life of what the proceeds were used to finance. For example, the repayment schedule for debt issued by a fire district to purchase a fire engine should attempt to match the useful life of the truck. A 30-year bond issue would be inappropriate if the engine's useful life is only 10 years. Likewise, an overdependence on short-term debt to finance longer-term projects can lead to serious liquidity problems, especially if interest rates were to rise significantly. Short-term borrowings, such as municipal notes (see Key 27), should normally be utilized by municipalities to meet seasonal borrowing needs.

Management and political factors. This broad category includes understanding how the governing bodies within a municipality are organized, and the interrelationship between these bodies. The political climate prevalent within a municipality must also be understood.

A strong executive branch of government—the mayor or governor—is generally preferred by analysts because this form of government can respond more expeditiously in the event of a fiscal crisis than a government controlled by a more fragmented body, such as a city council or state legislature. The default by the city of Cleveland on a G-O note issue in the late 1970s is often blamed on the extremely weak executive branch of its municipal government where incumbent mayors have limited fiscal powers and often focus more on getting elected every two years by meeting political demands, rather than on running the city effectively.

The credentials and experience of vital members of the municipality's decision-making bodies should be examined carefully. The financial viability of a municipality caught in a fiscal emergency could hinge upon the ability of a chief executive to react in a prompt and resourceful fashion.

Finally, the political climate of a municipality cannot be overlooked. The Orange County debacle taught us the importance of an issuer's *willingness to pay*. An adamant refusal to raise taxes on the part of Orange County citizens in order to repay bondholders could be traced to the anti-tax stance of Orange County's constituency.

31

REVENUE BONDS

Following the much-publicized Orange County debacle, much debate has been centered on the true strength of the much touted general obligation pledge (see Key 30). As a result, many conservative municipal investors are now taking a hard look at revenue bonds, once considered not as creditworthy as general obligation (G-O) bonds.

The revenue bond structure involves securing bonds with revenues generated from a specific project. Revenue, rather than taxing power, associated with G-Os is therefore pledged to repay bondholders. These revenues might take the form of user fees, tolls, rents, mortgage payments, or tuitions, which are normally paid by *users* of the facility constructed with the bond's proceeds. Special government entities, namely public revenue authorities, are often established to facilitate the issuance of revenue bonds.

Revenue bonds come in many varieties, including, but not limited to:

- *Health care bonds* to facilitate the construction of hospitals and other medical facilities
- *Higher education bonds* to aid in the building of universities and colleges
- *Water and wastewater bonds* to finance the construction of water and sewer systems
- *Housing bonds,* issued to finance the construction of both single- and multifamily housing units
- *Public power bonds,* issued to build electric utilities
- *Airport bonds* to finance the construction of the nation's airports

- *Resource recovery and solid waste bonds,* issued for the construction of facilities that convert waste into energy for ultimate sale. A separate Key will be dedicated to each of these bonds.

When looking at the creditworthiness of revenue bonds, the main focus of the analysis is on the bond's coverage, which denotes how much revenue is pledged to pay off the bond's principal and interest. From the revenue projected to be generated from a particular project, the forecasted operating expenses are deducted to arrive at the project's *net earnings*. How many times this net earnings amount covers debt service (the interest and principal that must be paid to debtholders each year) is the bond's coverage.

Project revenue × forecasted operating expenses
= net earnings.

Net earnings ÷ debt service = bond coverage

EXAMPLE:
  Given:
  Projected revenue = $20,000,000
  Operating expenses = $15,000,000
  Debt service = $4,000,000

  Then:
  Net earnings = $5,000,000
  Bond coverage = 1.25%

Revenues that are projected to be realized from this project after deducting operating expenses cover the amount that must be paid to debtholders 1.25 times.

The higher the coverage, the greater the cushion available to bondholders in the event that there is a shortfall in revenue, and/or unexpected increases in expenses. The adequacy of a bond's coverage must be considered in relation to the nature of the project. For example, a coverage of 1.25 times may be acceptable for a public utility (a monopoly) with a highly predictable revenue income, but unacceptable for a nursing home bond with highly erratic earnings.

Factors that Distinguish Revenue Bond Analysis from General Obligation Bond Analysis.

1. *Security provisions.* The backing for a revenue bond is generally narrower than that of a general obligation bond, because only income derived from a *specific* source is available to repay the bondholder. On the other hand, G-Os have a blanket pledge of the municipality's taxing power. Nonetheless, many investors find the revenue bond concept more straightforward and somewhat easier to comprehend. (If the project is viable and if it generates funds, there will be money to repay the bonds). The general obligation pledge (as seen in Key 53, The Three Debacles) is more obscure.

2. *Competition.* When analyzing revenue bonds, an extensive look at the project's competition is of the utmost importance; a competing service can drain precious income leading to financial problems for the issuer. For example, a toll road bond that is backed by tolls paid by users of the thoroughfare, would probably experience a severe financial setback if a free road were to be constructed nearby, particularly if it services a similar geographic region. It is imperative to ascertain whether the project is viable in the current competitive environment and whether it will remain so if other players emerge.

3. *Geographic area serviced.* How large is the geographic area that benefits from the service provided? The larger the area—several states—the less the project is susceptible to the economic cycles of a local community.

4. *Voter authorization.* This is not normally required for revenue bonds to be issued. The municipality thus has greater flexibility in accessing the capital markets than with G-Os that generally require a voter referendum.

5. *Bond indenture.* This specifies the legal rights and protections of the bondholder and the terms and

conditions of the offering. The rate covenant, or agreement, for instance, is a provision within the indenture that requires the issuer to raise rates (user fees) in a sufficient amount to repay principal and interest to the bondholder.

6. *Economic viability of the project.* The project being financed must make good business sense. The analysis of the Washington Public Power Supply System (WPPSS) debacle (see Key 53) illustrates the problems associated with a project that was not economically viable, for reasons that include cost overruns, insufficient demand for electricity, and others.

32

HIGHER EDUCATION BONDS

Even upper middle class parents who sock away a significant portion of their take-home pay each month, buying those zero coupon municipals discussed in Key 24, can't help but wonder: Will we be able to afford to send our children to college, not to mention graduate school? The tuition increases of higher education have virtually outpaced all other family costs, as well as increases in most incomes. A four-year college education has already proven prohibitively expensive for many families. If this tuition hyperinflation continues unabated, how many more deserving students will be priced out of the market? Investors in higher education bonds share this worry, since tuition receipts represent a large portion of most universities' total revenues that ultimately will provide the playback of principal and interest for the investor. The forecasting of tuition, similar to a corporation projecting sales, is the backbone of higher education bond analysis; however, it is only the beginning. Other factors to consider include the university's:

- prestige
- admissions policy
- endowment
- financial analysis

A university's prestige is a function of the credentials and reputation of both its faculty—degrees, publications, etc.—and students. While a highly valuable asset, it is nonetheless based on perception, because some little-known colleges with unpublished instructors may actually supply a more superior education. In addition, a university's prestige can be a fleeting commodity in the dynamic and competitive world of higher education. While some top Ivy League schools, such as Harvard and Yale, have remained at the apex of the university hierarchy through thick and thin, many other universities are in demand for the moment due to the popularity of specific program and student fads. A university's past success may not necessarily predict its future. The big question is: For whatever reason, will students still want to attend the college or university in the future?

The university's admission policy should be carefully scrutinized to ascertain its admissions flexibility. The lower a school's acceptance rate, the greater its admissions flexibility. For example, a college that accepts virtually every applicant will have a difficult time lowering its standards to increase matriculation. Conversely, a college that is very particular about whom it accepts (for instance, it accepts only 40 percent of the applicants), has a great deal of room to lower standards and still maintain a high-quality institution. As a rule, universities that accept over 75 percent of applicants can be considered lacking in the flexibility department.

The size of an institution's endowment is a strategic factor in its financial analysis, especially for private universities; state universities may have the state to lean on. An endowment is made up of restricted (the donor specifies what the money can be used for) and nonrestricted donations (the school can use the funds for whatever it wishes). While both are sought after, the nonrestricted endowment is preferable. Like money in the bank, it gives the institution greater financial flexibility and liquidity as well as aiding in its day-to-day operations.

When focusing on state-supported institutions, the political and economic climate of the home state must be considered as well. Fiscal and budget problems may force a reduction in state subsidies to these institutions, forcing greater reliance on tuition.

33

RESOURCE RECOVERY BONDS

What a brilliant business idea: taking garbage, converting it to energy, and then selling it! Resource recovery involves just that—the collection of garbage and other forms of waste products, transporting them to waste-to-energy facilities (WTE), where they are converted to energy and sold to utilities and other users of electricity. The popularity of resource recovery plants continues to grow in the United States for a number of reasons:

- the ever-increasing amounts of solid wastes that must be disposed of efficiently and economically
- the closing of existing landfills and the lack of availability of new sites
- past ecological damage and the government's response of stricter environmental standards for all forms of solid waste disposal
- a rise in the general cost of waste disposal, due largely to the above-mentioned, that has led to the search for alternative sources, such as resource recovery plants

The issuance of resource recovery bonds provides capital for the construction of waste-to-energy plants. The technological sophistication of resource recovery plants is only one of the many factors contributing to the highly complex nature of their analysis. In fact, a comprehensive analysis requires looking at the alternative revenue streams, the contracts entered into by the many players, the economy of the underlying service area, the plant itself, and resource recovery guarantees. It is truly a hybrid examination, combining both general obligation bond (see

Key 30) and corporate bond analysis into one. To aid in this process, the following format is recommended:

- understanding the project's unique structure
- analysis of revenue streams and relevant contracts
- examination of the resource recovery plant and its operations

Project structure. Investors must understand the complex structure of the resource recovery project, identifying the players, relevant contracts, customers, etc. While the structures of these projects vary, a common example would be as follows:

EXAMPLE:

A municipality forms an agency responsible for the hauling and disposal of garbage generated by the residents of the community. The agency, maintaining total say over all matters related to the disposal of solid waste, such as the fees charged, where garbage is hauled to, etc., decides that the community would be best served by the construction of a resource recovery plant. Bonds are floated by the *agency* with the proceeds lent to a firm responsible for the building and operation of the project. The agency agrees to deliver garbage and pay the associated disposal fees in a sufficient amount to enable the builder/operator to both run the plant and repay the bondholders' principal and interest.

In the case of insufficient deliveries of waste products and/or the noncompletion or nonoperation of the plant, the question arises of who is "guaranteeing" that bondholders will be repaid. In some cases, the municipality, or agency, must continue to pay tipping (disposal) fees for the life of the project, a put-or-pay contract. In other cases, the builder/operator guarantees payment of the debt service—the interest and principal payments.

Revenue Streams and Relevant Contracts. Revenues generated by resource recovery facilities are generally derived from two sources:

1. tipping (disposal) fees paid by the municipality and other deliverers of garbage, and

2. the sale of energy and other byproducts, such as scrap metal, of the resource recovery process to electric companies and other end users.

Tipping fees. These service fees are paid on a per ton basis, and generally account for a large percentage of a plant's overall revenue. The generation of tipping fees is a function of the amount of waste provided to the plant by the municipality. Therefore, a G-O-type analysis of the municipality supplying waste products must be undertaken. This analysis includes looking at population trends, income levels, the overall tax base, and other demographic factors. The very nature of a resource recovery plant lends itself to the classic NIMBY (not in my backyard) problem. While these plants continue to be constructed, despite the dissatisfaction of local residents, overall community support is seen as generally positive. In addition, the investor must determine:

- Will the municipality generate a sufficient amount of waste products to keep the plant busy full time?
- If not, will waste products delivered by other haulers supplement the municipality's garbage deliveries?
- Does the municipality have the legal right to require residents to utilize specific plants?
- Are the tipping fees competitively priced, as compared with competitive sources of waste disposal, and with tipping fees charged by neighboring communities?
- Are contracts between the municipality and the resource recovery plant valid and enforceable?

The sale of energy and other byproducts. A secondary source of revenue for the resource recovery plant is the income derived from the sale of electricity and other byproducts of the waste-to-energy process. An analysis similar to the one conducted in Key 38 (Public Power Bonds) must be performed to determine the overall market for energy produced by this process. Some of the questions to be answered are:

- Who are the current and potential purchasers of the energy?
- Do these buyers have the capacity, the financial ability, and the willingness to continue to purchase sufficient amounts of energy?
- Are the prices of the energy products regulated and/or competitive with other competing sources of energy?
- Are the contracts entered into with these energy buyers valid and enforceable ?

The Resource Recovery Plant. As with any proposed facility a feasibility study and/or engineer reports must be reviewed to determine the plant's likelihood of economic success. When evaluating the resource recovery plant, the following must be determined:

- Is the technology chosen: proven and viable, state of the art, cost efficient, etc.? For example, mass burning is considered as one of the most cost-effective and effective methods of converting waste to energy.
- Management's track record of managing resource recovery plants may provide a clue to future performance.
- What are the age, capacity, and condition of the facility, and what future capital improvements are required?
- Are there any proposed capital improvement plans, and what are the provisions for their financing?

The resource recovery bond's creditworthiness is only as strong as its weakest link. Due to the complexity in understanding the multitude of links, the investor is forced to rely on the rating agencies to a greater degree than normal. Investors are advised to purchase bonds rated A or better, and to diversify among several issuers.

34

WATER AND WASTEWATER BONDS

An analyst's dream revenue bond is one backed by user fees of a long established monopoly water system having significant control over its rates in a stable high wealth community. This contrived bond encompasses everything one looks for in a revenue bond: user fees based on a human necessity like water, an exclusive monopoly system that can raise prices if necessary, and users who can well afford the service.

Unfortunately, most water and wastewater bonds do not enjoy all the above-mentioned characteristics; however, as a general category of bonds, they are considered among the most creditworthy. In fact, analysts often rate a community's water bonds higher than the general obligation bonds of that same community. For example, New York City municipal water authority bonds are rated A by Moody's and A– by Standard & Poor's (A/A–) while NYC G-O debt is rated Baa1 by Moody's and BBB+ by Standard & Poor's (Baa1/BBB+).

When judging the creditworthiness of water bonds, the following must be considered:

- the service area economy
- revenue streams and other financial analysis
- management
- the water system

Analysts generally look for a growing population, rising income levels, and low unemployment rates. Overall, there must be a sufficient number of residents to support the system, and they must be residents who are able to afford the user fees charged by the authority. Rates charged to water system users must be compared to neighboring communities and to the general income levels of the citizenry of the service area. The reliance on a few major users is viewed as a negative. Analysts much prefer a diversified user base, made up of financially strong customers.

The revenue streams associated with water and wastewater bonds include flat rate and meter reading-based user charges, and connection and assessment fees. Analysts are most comfortable seeing revenue generated from user charges, because they are considered to be the most predictable. Connection fees, which are difficult to forecast, and the assessment fees, normally associated with proposed projects, are generally one-shot deals. Bonds with these fees as the primary source of income should maintain a greater financial cushion than those with user fees as the principal source of revenue.

The evaluation of the water authority's management, while highly subjective, focuses on some key issues. Here are a few.

- management's autonomy in setting user fees
- management's past success implementing changes on a timely basis
- whether management's past financial forecasts have proved reliable
- whether management has been able to implement the capital changes necessary to meet the stringent regulations proposed by both federal and state governments, such as the Safe Water Act and the Clean Water Act.

Potential investors should determine whether or not the latter changes have been implemented without the need for management to raise user fees to prohibitively expensive levels.

The physical water and wastewater system must be examined as well to determine its life span, physical state, storage and reserve capacity, and potential improvements. Costly changes might very well be involved if the system has not yet been modified to meet new government regulations.

When dealing with a proposed system, the analysis of water and wastewater begins to get complicated, especially in a new community. Analysts must answer the following questions:

- Will customers, currently using wells and septic tanks, switch to using the water and wastewater system?
- Will the community legally require residents to sign up with the new water system?
- Will enough families and companies ultimately move into the community?
- Is there a possibility of project delays and/or cost overruns?

Overall, water along with wastewater bonds represent high-quality municipal issues. Bonds rated A or better should undoubtedly be included as part of one's municipal portfolio.

35

HEALTH CARE (HOSPITAL) BONDS

Out of all the types of municipal bonds, health care bonds arguably subject the bondholder to the greatest amount of risk. Whenever a listing of problem bonds materializes—those being downgraded by the rating agencies or that are in default—health care bonds undoubtedly comprise a significant portion. They are extremely difficult to analyze and track and are known to deteriorate in quality as time passes. Major health care changes, continually being debated at all levels of government, threaten to further destabilize an already chaotic industry.

Health care bonds comprise a broad spectrum of institutions including: multihospital systems, which include several not-for-profit health care facilities that operate in concert, teaching hospitals, rehabilitation centers, psychiatric institutions, nursing homes, etc. The inherent risky nature of health care bonds mandates an extensive basic credit analysis. This analysis most resembles a corporate bond analysis, since a hospital is essentially a corporate enterprise. The ensuing credit analysis format can be used with other types of corporate-like revenue bonds as well.

Hospital Bond Credit Analysis.

Environment. Like a corporate bond analysis, investors must first look at the overall environment in which the health care facility operates. Wealth and income levels, projected population increases, level and diversification of industry (reliance on one major employer can pose serious problems if the firm leaves town or faces financial problems), and unemployment rates within the hospital's service area, are among the key demographic factors affecting the hospital's financial performance.

Hospitals do not, by any means, enjoy monopoly status like other municipal revenue bonds, such as water and sewer bonds. Competition in the health care industry is fierce for qualified staff—doctors and administrative personnel—advanced medical technologies, and patients. This competition is mitigated to some extent by the vital nature of health care—people now more than ever seem overly concerned with their health—and with the aging "baby boomers" supplying a constant stream of new customers to our nation's hospitals. A community's demand for a new or existing health care facility is vital to the viability of that hospital. Building a hospital in an area that is already saturated with health care facilities is a surefire prescription for disaster. A prosperous hospital must have the ability to continually attract a sufficient flow of patients from the local (primary service) area as well as neighboring areas (secondary service area).

Management. The experience and competency of the hospital's management is of critical importance in evaluating its creditworthiness. While past performance is no guarantee of future success, it is nonetheless a good place to begin. Management's past success in budgeting effectively, employee relations, developing a strategic niche (area of expertise), settling litigation, etc., are all indicative of management's ability to run the hospital efficiently and effectively.

Operations. The investor must understand the factors influencing the health care facility's revenues and costs.

The prohibitive cost of health care in the United States today has led most families to rely on private health insurers and/or the federal government (Medicare and/or Medicaid) to pay most of their medical and hospital bills. In fact, the lion's share of revenues of most hospitals comes from reimbursement from these private insurers and the government (*third party reimbursement*). As costs to hospitals continue to climb, a serious problem faces hospitals: These third party reimbursers are spending considerable time and money mounting campaigns to limit the amount of money paid to hospitals. States too are attempting to do their part in controlling medical costs by limiting payments to hospitals.

Costs, incurred by these health care facilities, on the other hand, are allowed to rise totally unregulated. The end result is often a financial squeeze on those hospitals lacking the financial flexibility to deal with this unfavorable environment. A hospital with a high cost structure relative to competing hospitals is seen as possessing a major competitive disadvantage.

Liquidity analysis. Liquidity analysis involves determining how quickly a health care facility, or any corporate enterprise, can come up with "hard cash" if needed. Various ratios (ratio analysis) are used to help investors gauge a hospital's ability to come up with the money needed to pay the bills. The *current ratio* is among the most valuable ratios used to assess liquidity. It is calculated by dividing the institution's current liabilities— what is owed during this fiscal year—into its current assets, such as marketable securities, accounts receivable, etc., which can be converted into cash relatively quickly, displaying how many times current assets can cover what is owed in the near future. A superior, compared to competing hospitals, and rising current ratio indicates the ability to raise cash to weather a short-term budget crisis.

Leverage (debt levels). The investor must determine if the health care facility has borrowed too extensively and whether it can repay its existing debt, especially during financially trying times.

Financial ratios used in determining proper debt levels include the *debt service coverage ratio* and the *long-term debt to equity ratio*:

The debt service coverage ratio is calculated by taking the hospital's net income, adding back the depreciation expense (a noncash charge) and dividing that figure by total annual principal and interest payments (current or projected). It tells the investor how many times the cash flow generated by the hospital covers money owed to creditors. For example, a debt service coverage ratio of 2 means that the hospital can cover total debt service by 2× (times). This figure, once again, should be viewed over time and compared to the debt service coverage ratios of other hospitals.

By dividing the hospital's long-term debt into total equity (net worth), we can ascertain the debt-to-equity ratio. A lower ratio, evidencing more suitable debt levels, is preferred by analysts.

Additional factors. Consider these other factors:

- *Breakdown of physicians.* The doctors' credentials, such as educational background and board certification, their ages, and areas of expertise, are vital in appraising the quality of any hospital.
- *Market niche.* Investors must look at the health care facility's mix of services. A hospital that specializes in one particular medical area (Sloan Kettering is renowned as a cancer treatment center, for instance) has a competitive advantage in attracting patients, albeit, a less diversified "customer base."
- *Type of health care facility.* The type of health care facility must be considered as well. This diverse group of institutions, lumped together under one heading, vary widely in their crediworthiness. Nursing homes, for instance, often top the list of "troubled" bonds. A small rural hospital in a depressed area of the country is most likely financially worse off than a teaching hospital that is affiliated with a renowned medical school and located in a affluent community.
- *Proposed or newly constructed health care facility.* With a new or proposed hospital, a feasibility study must be examined carefully. A feasibility study, normally prepared by an outside consultant, attempts to ascertain (project) whether the hospital is needed, whether it can be financially viable, and, ultimately, and most importantly to the bondholder, if it will be able to repay its debt.

The future of the health care industry will undoubtedly be characterized by continued consolidations and mergers to gain greater operating efficiency. With national health care debates continuing to threaten revenue sources for hospitals, investors are urged more than ever to be careful!

36

HOUSING BONDS

Of all the types of municipal bonds, housing bonds are issued with the noblest of intentions: to create and preserve affordable housing nationwide. They can be broken down into two general categories: single-family housing bonds and multifamily housing bonds. Each of these types of housing bonds maintain distinct structures and characteristics.

Single-Family Housing Bonds. Single-family housing bonds have helped make home ownership a dream come true for many families. Tax-exempt bonds are issued by mortgage agencies (state agencies) throughout the country, with proceeds directed toward low and moderate income families purchasing single-family homes. A single-family home, as defined by the federal government, includes: one- to four-family houses, condominiums, and co-ops. In the case of multifamily dwellings, the borrower must reside in one of the dwellings for the life of the mortgage. The tax-free status of the bonds issued allows the housing agencies to borrow at low tax-free rates, and then turn around and supply below market (low interest rate) mortgages to qualified applicants. The federal government, through the Internal Revenue Service, mandates the requirements to receive these favored mortgages causing us to wonder, "Who are the qualified applicants?" For example, only first-time home buyers are eligible for mortgage agency loans. In addition, there is a requirement regarding the purchase price of the dwelling (for an existing one-family house in Long Island, New York, for instance, the maximum price of a home is $165,500) and the maximum income that can be earned by the borrower. The last thing the government wants is for a millionaire to build a mansion with federally subsidized mortgage rates!

Investors purchasing these single-family housing bonds not only help to promote a public good, but receive high tax-free income with a generally strong backing (if the correct housing bonds are purchased).

What backs (secures) single-family housing bonds?

- The primary source of repayment for holders of single-family housing bonds are the mortgage payments made by the homebuyers. Each monthly payment made by the homebuyer, covering principal and interest, flows back to the bondholders, paying interest and principal on their bonds. The mortgages, generally insured by a private insurer, or an agency of the federal government, such as the Federal Housing Administration (FHA) or the Government National Mortgage Association (GNMA), are pledged as collateral to the bondholder. Housing bonds with federal government backing, are normally rated higher by the rating agencies (AAA) than those with backing by private insurers.

- As with most revenue bonds, various reserve funds are set up. For example, a housing agency issuing $100 million in bonds, may lend out only $90 million, keeping $10 million in reserve. In the event of a deficiency in cash flow, where not enough money is available from homebuyers to repay bondholders, the agency can dip into these reserve funds to repay bondholders.

As an example of what process occurs when a borrower (homeowner) defaults on the mortgage, the following procedure exists for conducting the State of New York Mortgage Agency (SONYMA):

1. Upon default by the homeowner, the housing agency immediately takes title to the property.
2. The agency then approaches the private mortgage insurer. Note: Individuals that borrow a large percentage of the value of the home are required to take out private mortgage insurance. The private insurer must then ante up a certain percentage of the home's value.
3. The agency then sells the property.
4. The agency appeals to the pool insurer for any deficiency in the amount realized by the sale. Pool insurers are wholesale underwriters who insure the entire pool of mortgages up to a certain stop-loss amount. Normally, pool insurers are called upon to pay a relatively small percentage of the total loan. In fact, even

during the real estate collapse in Texas during the early 1970s, claims made upon pool insurers rarely reached the stop-loss amount.

Multifamily Housing Bonds. With multifamily housing bonds, proceeds from the issuance of tax-exempt bonds are lent out to real estate developers, who construct multifamily apartment buildings.

The federal government mandates that a certain percentage of the apartments be set aside to benefit low and moderate income families who receive rent subsidies. While the percentages vary, a common structure is the 80/20 deal. Here, the government tells the developer that "in order to receive tax-advantaged financing (lower mortgage rate) 20 percent of apartment units in a particular structure must be rented at below market value to those of low and moderate incomes. The other 80 percent can be rented at whatever price the market bears, to whomever can afford the price."

The bondholder's primary source of repayment are the mortgage payments. As with single-family bonds, principal and interest payments on the mortgage are used to repay bondholders. Since the bonds are ultimately secured by this underlying mortgage, their creditworthiness is determined to a large degree by what party is insuring the mortgage. Third party mortgage insurers include:

- *The federal government.* Through governmental bodies such as the Federal Housing Administration (FHA) and the Veterans Housing Authority (VHA), the federal government secures the mortgages made on various multifamily housing mortgages. Bonds backed by federally insured mortgages are among the highest rated municipal securities, generally receiving an AAA rating.
- *State housing agencies.* In addition to issuing bonds on behalf of developers, state housing agencies are often called upon to secure the underlying mortgage as well. This practice amounts to a moral guarantee on the part of the state, as any shortfall in funds targeted for bondholder repayment would have to be appropriated by the state legislature. While generally not AAA-rated, rating agencies, nonetheless, look favorably upon this form of backing. Bonds in this category often receive AA ratings.

- *Private insurers.* Private insurers, including banks and insurance companies, insure underlying mortgages as well. While normally not as creditworthy as federal and state guarantees, private insurers may provide adequate protection to bondholders. The official statement (see Key 55) contains complete information about the private insurer.

As with single-family housing bonds, multifamily bonds maintain reserve funds as well. These reserves are used for shortfalls in funds needed to repay bondholders (the debt service reserve fund, for example, contains an amount equal to one year's principal and interest payments), as well as for maintenance and repairs of the apartment buildings.

Investors purchasing single- and multifamily housing bonds should stick to insured mortgage bonds. These bonds should be rated A or better by the rating agencies. Under no circumstances should the neophyte investor purchase an unrated and/or uninsured housing bond.

Investors should also be cognizant of *special housing calls,* which are extraordinary calls (see Key 23). From funds borrowed by housing agencies and not lent out to homebuyers and developers (unexpended proceeds), housing agencies, are allowed to call bonds, normally at par, prior to maturity. In addition, as borrowers sell their existing homes, and refinance their mortgages, subsequently repaying the agencies, these agencies may again call in bonds prematurely. These are called prepayment calls.

Investors purchasing housing bonds in the aftersale market should be especially careful when paying a premium for the bonds. Paying a significant amount over par, for example, $110,000 for a $100,000 face value, could lead to a significant loss should the bonds be called soon after. However, there is a classification of housing bonds that are structured so that large amounts of bonds will indeed be called each year. These bonds are called *Super Sinkers.*

Super Sinkers. Super Sinkers, associated with single-family housing issues, involve a unique financial structure that mandates that the issuer use all funds from early mortgage prepayments of a particular bond issue to retire bonds of a specific *maturity* of that same issue. Term bonds, or long

111

maturities, are normally the bonds that are targeted as Super Sinkers. Like Ginnie Maes, a Super Sinker's average life may be far shorter than its stated maturity, as portions of the investor's principal may be returned each year as the underlying mortgages are prepaid. The average maturity of a particular Super Sinker cannot be exactly known, but can only be estimated based upon past prepayment performance, or prior experience.

When sold in the new issue market, Super Sinkers are normally priced (sold) at par or at a discount. When purchasing these bonds in the resale market, the investor should again attempt to purchase these securities at par, at a discount, or at a very marginal premium. As explained above, when dealing with special housing calls and/or sinking funds, investors should avoid paying substantial premiums. With Super Sinkers, this rule takes on even more importance, as the chances of early calls, by design, are greatly enhanced.

37

STUDENT LOAN BONDS

Anyone who has applied for a government student loan when entering college cannot easily forget the time and energy expended filling out forms and other paperwork. At the same time, one also remembers the favorable interest rate and hopefully superb education obtained during this period. Likewise, investors who dedicate the time and energy to understanding the complex structure of student loan bonds will be amply rewarded in the form of a relatively high return, considering the risk undertaken.

In the early 1960s the U.S. federal government, through its Department of Education (DOE), took on the job of helping to promote higher education by *guaranteeing principal and interest on student loans properly originated and serviced*. This was the beginning of the creation of the student loan bond, which if properly structured, can offer the investor a stellar credit backing (quasi U.S. government backing), and returns that normally exceed "pure vanilla" municipal bonds, such as G-O bonds with similar ratings.

The Process of Obtaining a Student Loan. To create a student loan:

1. The student applies for the government-guaranteed student loan with a participating bank by filling out and submitting the appropriate loan applications.
2. If properly applied for pursuant to the Education Act, and approved, the loan becomes eligible for the Federal Finance Education Loan Program (FFELP) and the ultimate guarantee by the DOE (U.S. federal government).

3 While in school, interest on the loan is paid to the lending bank

- by the U.S. government for students from low income homes. Following graduation or leaving school, these students receive a six-month grace period where the government continues to pay interest on the debt.
- by the students themselves if from higher income households.

4. Following the grace period, or graduation, in the case of students from higher income homes, the student is faced with repaying the loan. The student must repay the loan in equal payment amounts over seven years (level principal amortization) at an interest rate that fluctuates in line with the 91-day Treasury bill yield, a below market interest rate. The government may once again enter the picture with an allowance paid to the lending bank that supplements the payment made by the student borrower.

5. Servicing of these student loans is quite expensive and time-consuming. Since the sale of these loans will free up capital for other more lucrative endeavors, the lending bank may decide that it no longer wishes to keep the student loan on its books. Consequently, the bank will sell the student loan to the appropriate state-endorsed Student Loan Authority, whose function is to promote secondary education by purchasing existing student loans and/or lending money directly to students, thus originating the loans.

The Student Loan Bond. The Student Loan Authority issues student loan bonds to raise the funds necessary to purchase loans from originating banks and/or to lend funds directly to students. These bonds are sold to the public as either normal fixed coupon bonds, or as auction rate securities structured in a similar fashion as municipal auction preferred stock (see Key 28).

EXAMPLE:

The Mississippi Student Loan Authority issues $50,000,000 of student loan bonds. With the money raised from the bond sale it:

- lends the funds directly to students desiring to attend one of Mississippi's esteemed schools of higher education; and/or
- identifies the $50,000,000 in existing student loans that banks seek to remove from their books matching the payment structure of the bonds issued. The authority subsequently purchases these loans from interested banks. Remember, the payment of interest and repayment of the underlying student loan is needed to pay the interest and principal on the bond issue.

The student loans themselves, and the cash flow generated by the repayment of the loans, are generally pledged to Mississippi Student Loan bondholders. As students make their interest and principal payments, the funds ultimately flow through to pay interest and principal on the bonds held by investors. If the primary source of repayment—what backs the bonds—on student loan bonds are the loan payments made by those who have borrowed money for college, some of whom have not found jobs, or are underemployed, why are they generally considered of superior credit quality? To explain why, we must introduce two additional players into our analysis: the intermediary guarantor, and the Department of Education (DOE).

Every student loan under the FFELP program is guaranteed by an intermediary guarantor, a state-endorsed entity. In the case of a default on any student loan underlying the student loan bond, the intermediary guarantor takes on the responsibility of processing the default claims by initially paying the bondholder the total amount in default (shortage of funds). The guarantor then turns to the federal government (Department of Education) to be reimbursed for the vast majority of the amount expended. Prior to 1993 the loans were 100 percent guaranteed by the federal government. Congress, however, recently changed the law, insuring qualified student loans at only 98 percent of value. The federal government is thus where the buck once again stops, since it is the ultimate guarantor of the bonds.

Student loan bonds possess complicated financial structures and cash flows. Investors should understand the potential for a disruption or shortage of these cash flows due to excessive delinquencies and defaults, and whether reserve funds are able to generate satisfactory interest income to offset these contingencies. Investors are urged to purchase *only* issues rated A or better by Moody's and/or Standard & Poor's. Among its other credit review procedures, the rating agencies will confirm that the bond issue is legally structured, that bondholders have first lien on the underlying student loans, and that loans are in fact bona fide U.S. government-backed student loans.

38

PUBLIC POWER BONDS

The Public Power Act of 1930, promulgated by Congress to help electrify sparsely populated areas of our vast country, is the forebear of the Public Power Authority. Through public power authorities, utilities are able to borrow tax free to help generate, disburse, and sell electric power. Although issuing a massive quantity of municipal bonds, these public power authorities account for a surprisingly small percentage of total power produced in the United States—roughly 15 percent of total power sales. The majority of the total production—roughly 75 percent—is generated by private utilities, such as Long Island Lighting, Niagara Mohawk, etc., with the balance produced by the federal government, as through the Tennessee Valley Authority.

Municipal bonds are issued by four basic types of public utilities:

1. utilities that generate strictly power
2. utilities that distribute strictly power
3. utilities that both generate and distribute power
4. joint action agencies

Utilities that Generate Strictly Power. These public utility systems act solely as producers and wholesalers of electric power. The New York State Power Authority, which is one of the largest public power agencies in the United States, is an excellent example of a power producer/wholesaler. Tax-exempt bonds are sold to the investing public, with the proceeds directed toward the construction and/or expansion of power plants. The electricity generated by these plants is generally sold to privately owned utilities, such as Niagara Mohawk and Con Edison, rather than to the end users of the power, such as individual households.

Utilities that Distribute Strictly Power. These public utility systems do not own or construct power plants, and thus cannot generate power. They act solely in the capacity of a distributor, purchasing power from the creators of electricity, and subsequently distributing the power within its service area. National Tennessee Municipal Electric System is a good example of a power distributor. Electric power is purchased primarily from the Tennessee Valley Authority (TVA), which was created by the U.S. government in 1933 to (among other things) generate and sell electrical power to various municipalities within the region, and is subsequently sold to its own customers, such as homeowners and factories.

Utilities that Generate and Distribute Power. These public utility systems generate as well as distribute electric power to the end users. Tax-exempt bonds are thus issued for the construction of power plants and distribution networks. Los Angeles County, California; Seattle, Washington; and Orlando, Florida, are among the municipalities that construct and operate their own generating plants and, at the same time, sell the power produced to the final consumer.

Joint-Action Agencies. These types of agencies are comprised of a group of municipal electric systems that join together for the purpose of issuing bonds for the building of generating stations and/or for buying into existing generating plants. By joining forces, these utilities hope to realize significant economies of scale, borrowing funds at more advantageous rates, and more efficiently and cost effectively generating and distributing electric power. One of the largest joint-action agencies in the United States—and incidentally one of the largest issuers of tax-exempt debt—is the Intermountain Power Agency of Utah (IPA). A brief discussion of this agency follows.

Intermountain Power Agency, Utah. As a way to decrease their dependence on oil to generate electricity, various public utilities, primarily from the Southern California region, joined together to form the Intermountain Power Agency. The agency's mandate was to utilize Utah's vast coal deposits as an added source of power in the region. Roughly 90 percent of the total energy output produced by the IPA is sold in California, with the lion's share distributed in Los Angeles, Anaheim, and Riverside, California (Southern California). In fact, only a small percentage of total output is sold in Utah. Massive amounts of bonds are issued by the IPA, with the proceeds targeted toward this large-scale power production. Economies of scale have led to a more cost-effective approach to energy production.

Prior to purchasing public power bonds, investors must evaluate the following:

- the type of project
- the demand for power in the particular service area
- financial factors
- contracts

Type of Project. Understanding the type of project being financed is the first step in the analysis of power bonds. For example, investors must be able to differentiate between a generating system and a transmission, or distribution system. Furthermore, the method by which power is produced—coal, nuclear, hydroelectric, etc.—is an important factor in the credit evaluation procedure. Some forms of power are safer, more cost-efficient, and environmentally friendly than others. For example, hydroelectric power is generally regarded as the most cost-efficient power source. Nuclear power, once regarded as the savior of America's power systems, has become increasingly more expensive. Higher regulatory and design modification costs, following the Three-Mile Island debacle, resulted in less cost-effective power production than originally anticipated.

Analysts generally look for a diversified fuel mix. A shortage of a certain fuel may lead to dire consequences for the power agency that relies solely on one particular source of energy.

The Demand for Power. The demand for electricity within the utility's service area is at the heart of the credit analysis of power bonds. Investors should look for service areas with growing populations, employment and income levels, and industrial activity. The customer base should be diversified among residential, commercial, and industrial users of power. No one end user should account for a disproportionately large share, greater than 10 percent, for example, of total energy sold. An over-reliance on one or several large customers can spell disaster if these firms decide to leave the area or fall on hard times. Overall, investors must determine whether there is sufficient demand for power within the service area to support the project.

In the case of a proposed facility and/or the expansion of an existing one, a feasibility study—projection of anticipated revenues and costs, engineering reports, etc.—must be conducted and reviewed. This report can assist analysts in determining if the project makes economic sense.

Financial Factors. The revenue derived from the sale of electricity is what generally secures, or backs, public power bonds. Thus, it is this revenue, after deducting operating expenses (net revenue) that is pledged to be used to repay bondholders' principal and interest. Investors must therefore look at the trends of revenue growth, over the past five years, for instance, as well as how this net revenue covers the debt service. In other words, after deducting all operating expenses from the income received from energy sales, how far does this sum go in paying off debtholders? Coverage ratios for power utilities generally range from 1 to 1.5 times. Due to the predictable nature of revenue flows, analysts normally view a 1 times coverage (net revenue = debt service) as a minimum acceptable level of debt coverage. Investors are advised to look at the trend in the coverage ratio over time, as well as in comparison to similar power projects.

A rate covenant, a legal requirement disclosed in the bond indenture, requires agencies to set rates high enough so that revenue is able to cover interest and principal payments. Rates charged for power must be competitive with other sources of energy. Utilities should have the ability to raise rates quickly without regulatory approval, in response to an unanticipated increase in costs.

Contracts. There are basically two types of contracts relating to power projects: take-or-pay and take-and-pay. A take-or-pay contract requires participants in a joint action agency—those municipal utilities that join together—to pay for their share of power costs, whether or not power is ever produced in the event that the power plant is never completed or temporarily shut down, for example.

A take-and-pay contract requires participants to pay for power only when it is available. The validity and enforceability of the various contracts signed is of vital importance to analysts and investors.

Readers are urged to read the section in Key 53 pertaining to the Washington Public Power Supply System (WPPSS) at this time. The WPPSS debacle is a case study of how Murphy's Law (in which everything that can go wrong, will!) applies to the public power bond arena.

39

AIRPORT BONDS

The expansion of airports in both number and size throughout our country over the past several decades to meet increased demand for air travel brought a major need for financing these enormous expenditures. Tax-exempt airport bonds filled this need as grants by the federal government proved insufficient to pay for this phenomenal growth.

In 1978, with the passing of the Airline Deregulation Act, came a fundamental change in the way airport revenue bonds were viewed and analyzed by market participants. This act granted airlines more flexibility regarding the setting of prices and routes, and increased competition among airlines, thereby creating a more market-driven industry. As a result, many airlines began to feel the financial pressures associated with deregulation.

These pressures, exacerbated by recessionary cycles in the nation's economy, led to the bankruptcy of some major carriers and the continued malaise and consolidation in the airline industry. It thus became imperative for investors in airport bonds to become corporate bond experts—as they relate to the airline industry. Investors must understand the specific financial and economic problems of airline carriers in this new competitive environment.

While airport debt comes in many varieties, the most popular form is the General Airport Revenue Bond (GARB). A GARB is generally backed by the net revenues, such as landing fees charged by airports to airlines each time a plane utilizes one of its runways, lease payments for use of hangers and terminals, concession revenue, and other related services, minus operating and maintenance costs. Investors should also consider the following, prior to investing.

The underlying economy. In analyzing the airport's economic base, it is important to review such local demographics as population trends in the local economy, the viability and diversity of industry, per capita income, unemployment levels, and other influences. The strength of the local economy is sure to influence the performance of most airports.

Feasibility, or past performance of the facility. In the case of a new or expanding facility, estimates of projected revenue and costs as well as economic and engineering reports must be reviewed. For existing airports, past financial performance may provide a clue to the future stability of operations. In both cases, it must be determined if there is sufficient demand for the services of the airport.

Overall, the investor should consider whether the building, expansion, or continued operation of the airport make good business sense.

The management and administration of the airport facility. In the United States most airports are owned and operated by local governments through government corporations. For example, the Port Authority of New York and New Jersey (government corporation), operates the major airports in New York and New Jersey—Kennedy, La Guardia, and Newark. Managers of our nation's airports must be evaluated on their ability to balance budgets, respond to a crisis, negotiate contracts with unions, motivate employees, and achieve financial goals. In addition, the administrative structure of the airport must be analyzed to ascertain the degree of control, and financial flexibility mandated to those who run our country's airport systems.

The following unique characteristics of GARBs must be considered as well:

1. *Is the airport in question Origin-and-Destination (O&D) in nature, or a Hub-and-Spoke (H&S) system?*

    An airport is considered to be *Origin-and-Destination* in nature when the majority of passengers use it for their place of ultimate destination, or for their initial departure. A *Hub-and-Spoke system*

123

involves the airport being a transfer point for passengers between connecting flights. All things being equal, H&S airports are considered riskier than O&D airports, because the former is normally dependent on one or two major airline carriers for the bulk of its revenue. If one of these private airline companies falls on hard times, another carrier may not be available to replace it and make up the lost income. Origin-and-Destination airports, on the other hand, are less dependent on the particular air carriers serving them; their income stream is significantly more diversified. Therefore, the success of an O&D airport is tied, to a considerable degree, to the strength of the area's economy and to the number of potential passengers within that local economy.

2. *What type of revenue stream is associated with the particular airport system, residual or compensatory?*

The important distinctions between a residual and compensatory system is whether the airport or the airline carrier assumes the majority of the financial risk.

With a *residual* structure, successful operations are virtually guaranteed by the airline carrier, since rates charged to the airlines are set so that a minimum "break-even" is incurred by the airport facility. Regardless of how many passengers travel through the airport or utilize the facilities, the airline must pay up!

The financial burden is thus shifted, to a large degree, to the airlines and away from the airport system. For this guarantee, the airline receives reduced user fees, such as terminal rental and landing fees, and shares in the revenue generated by concessions and other revenue sources, and maintains a voice in what capital expenditures will be completed by the airport system.

With a *compensatory* structure, the airport assumes the financial burden, allocating to the airline only those direct costs associated with the space used by the airline in day-to-day operations.

As a result of this structure, the airline has little or no voice in the capital expenditures made by the airport and will not share in the revenue generated by concessions and other non-airline-related income.

From the investor's standpoint the residual rate structure is preferable, since the airlines and not the airport—nor the holders of airport bonds—have the greatest degree of financial risk.

40

WHO ARE THE PLAYERS IN THE MUNICIPAL MARKET?

In the attempt to funnel money from investors seeking to lend their funds to those municipalities seeking to borrow, and subsequently to assure a somewhat liquid resale market, a large number of players emerge. The participants, all of which are vital to this endeavor include:

1. *Investors*—individual investors, mutual funds, investment advisors, insurance companies, corporations, and bank trust departments.

2. *Bond salespeople*—individuals who interface with the investors. They are normally broken down into retail and institutional groups based on the type of investor they service. In addition to selling bonds and servicing the customers' accounts, the salesperson is often relied on to provide market input to the traders and underwriters.

3. *Traders*—individuals who take positions and make markets in municipal bonds. In other words, these people agree to buy and sell various securities. Similar to a retail store's merchandiser, the trader's job is to decide what bonds to buy and to service the salesman's—and ultimately the investor's—needs. In addition, traders often buy on spec, anticipating that bonds purchased will appreciate in price, due primarily to falling interest rates or an improvement in the bond's credit quality, and can then be sold at higher prices to investors or other dealers.

4. *Underwriters*—individuals who bring new issues to market. When a municipality needs to borrow funds, it is the underwriter who decides how to price the bond issue—what yields to offer. It is truly a balancing act in both pleasing investors who are seeking the highest return, and issuers looking to pay the lowest rate possible.
5. *Municipal analysts*—individuals who look at wealth levels, economic trends, debt burdens, and other factors that help in ascertaining a municipality's financial health. The analyst may be called upon to approve a bond issue prior to the actual sale of the security.
6. *Investment bankers*—the dealmakers, who interface with the issuers, structuring bond deals that are ultimately sold to the investing public.
7. *Bond trustee*—the bank appointed as a fiduciary whose primary responsibility is protecting the bondholder by compelling the issuer to abide by the terms of the bond contract.
8. *Paying agent*—the bank that makes the interest and principal payments to the holders of the bonds.
9. *Bond counsels*—the lawyers who give the legal opinions, attesting to the bond's tax-exempt status and compliance with current bond law.

41

SELECTING A MUNICIPAL BOND BROKER

Selecting a munibond broker, the person selling municipal bonds, is probably the single most important decision an investor will make concerning municipal bond investing. One cannot help relying heavily on this market professional. Brokers have at their fingertips a research department, a vast array of research materials, information systems, and, potentially, years of experience. They may also have a great deal of input into the offering price of the bond.

What to Look for in a Broker.

1. *Municipal bond specialist.* An investor should seek out a broker whose area of expertise is fixed-income investing or investing in bonds. Furthermore, the broker should specialize in tax-free bonds. There are many brokers who are generalists (glorified stockbrokers), with municipal bonds just one of many products they sell. They often have little knowledge of the complexities of the municipal bond market, and in the event a problem arises, they may be of little or no assistance to the investor.

2. *Attitude toward risk.* Investors should look for a broker who has a similar attitude toward risk. Some firms specialize in high-grade conservative issues, while others deal in high-yield junk bonds (see Key 25). Similarly, individual brokers have varying attitudes toward the risk/reward tradeoff. If an investor is defensive, seeking safety as a principal investment objective, it is important to deal with a conservative bond broker. If one's primary objective is maximization of return, with less emphasis on the safety of the principal (a

strategy not recommended), an aggressiv
be acceptable.

3. *Brokers that consistently offer the highe
est prices*). It is imperative that the m
investor shop around prior to purchasir
Unlike the Treasury market, where sec
normally quoted in various periodicals,
quotes are difficult, if not impossible,
checking with several firms, the investo
yield to maturities on similar bonds, pu
bonds with the highest returns. If one
tently offers superior bonds at attractive
be wise to develop a relationship, demon
degree of loyalty. You may be rewarded b
all service and by being the broker's first
"hot" bonds become available.

4. *Discount brokers*. Do not assume that disco
are the answer to municipal investing problem
many discount brokers do an excellent job, the hete
neous nature of municipal bonds may not lend its
this type of service. While buying 100 shares of IBI
a relatively simple process when dealing with a disco
broker, the complexities of the municipal market m
require a degree of expertise not available in many firm
Further, many brokerage houses are neither new-issu
participants, nor secondary market makers. As a result,
the bonds they offer may not be attractively priced.

How to Find a Bond Broker.

1. *Word of mouth*. Approach acquaintances who may be
sophisticated investors and whose judgment you
respect.

2. *Financial and business professionals*. Speak to accountants, lawyers, investment advisors, and other financial
professionals.

3. *Banks*. Approach your bank to see if they have a municipal bond dealership department.

4. *Recommendations*. Speak with the office manager of a
major brokerage house for recommendations of a broker who specializes in tax-free bonds.

42

THE PRIMARY
(NEW ISSUE) MARKET

...mary market is where municipalities go to raise
... their many financial needs, such as building a
... bridge, or buying a school bus or fire engine.
... estors buy bonds in the primary market, they
... ect, lending money to cities, towns, school dis-
... for these various purposes. This contrasts with
... dary market where investors purchase existing
... rom other investors.

... he financial structure of municipal new issues is
... que from that of other fixed-income securities, such as
... easuries and corporate bonds, in that they are nor-
... ally comprised of a series of maturities (a serial issue).
... Rather than borrowing funds to be repaid in one single
(bullet) payment, say in 20 years, municipal loans are
normally repaid in a series of payments spread out over
many years. This financial structure tends to ease the
financial burden of having to come up with a massive
sum to be repaid all at once. The following is a sample of
a municipal bond new issue scale.

EXAMPLE:
> *Total issue size:* $1,000,000
> *Issuer:* Village of Highland Falls, Orange County,
>   New York
> *Insured:* AMBAC
> *Moody's:* Aaa
> *S&P:* AAA
> *Dated:* 02/01/96
> *First coupon:* 08/01/96
> *Due:* 02/01
> *Expected settlement:* 2/09/96

Amount	Maturity	Coupon	Basis	Price
200,000	02/01/97	5.00%	3.60%	101.33
200,000	02/01/98	5.00%	3.80%	102.26
200,000	02/01/99	5.00%	4.00%	102.78
200,000	02/01/00	5.00%	4.10%	103.27
200,000	02/01/01	5.00%	4.20%	103.56

The Village of Highland Falls in Orange County, New York, needs to borrow $1,000,000 for various capital projects (issuing $1,000,000 in bonds). The bonds are insured by the AMBAC Insurance Corporation and consequently rated Aaa/AAA. Since the bonds are dated (issued as of) February 1, 1996, the issuer must start paying interest as of that day. Since the first coupon date is August 1, 1996, the purchaser will receive the first interest payment on that date.

The expected settlement date is February 9, 1996, the day when the initial purchaser must pay for the bonds.

The village is selling $200,000 face value of bonds maturing each February 1 from 1997 to 2001. There is an identical coupon rate of 5 percent set on all the bonds. The yield to maturities and their corresponding prices are quoted for each maturity. Note how the yield rises as the maturity date gets farther out (upward sloping yield curve, see Key 9).

Now that we see what a new issue scale looks like, we can discuss the actual underwriting of municipal bonds.

Underwriting Municipal Bonds. Underwriting, or the process by which municipal bond dealers purchase the bond issue from the municipality, in effect, lending the dealer's funds to the municipality, and then resell it to investors, hopefully at a profit, can take on various forms. The two most common are the *competitive* and the *negotiated* underwriting.

Competitive underwriting. This involves the formation of several competing groups of dealers that join forces for the purpose of purchasing a bond issue from a municipality and then reselling it to investors. These groups or syndicates submit bids to the issuer, indicating at what yields and prices the issue can be sold to the investing public. The syndicate with the lowest interest cost bid is normally awarded the issue; the lower the interest rate the issuer pays, the better. Municipalities are often required by law, especially when issuing general obligation bonds, to solicit competing bids from various dealers for their securities. It is arguably felt that competitive bidding leads to the lowest interest rates for the issuing municipality.

Negotiated underwriting. In a negotiated underwriting, the municipality chooses a lead underwriter from various candidates. The job of this underwriter is to structure the bond deal. This involves deciding over how many years the loan will be repaid, how much will be repaid each year, and when and if the bonds can be called by the issuer. This underwriter generally has major input into what yields will be offered to investors. The lead underwriter then brings in other dealers to form a negotiated syndicate whose function it is to set the appropriate yield returns, or "price the issue," and then sell the securities to the investing public. It is truly a balancing act between pleasing the issuer, who is seeking the lowest borrowing cost and the investors who are looking for the highest available rate of return. If not pleased, the issuer can take his/her future business elsewhere. Some market participants complain that negotiating an issue removes the competitive pressure, and thus results in higher interest costs for the issuer and ultimately the taxpayer. Advocates of the negotiated process, however, make the argument that municipalities receive better and more customized service, expertise in structuring unique and complex deals, and better terms (lower rates) on large issues. This is especially true when dealing with issuers of a very low credit standing who at one time may have lost access to the public markets, such as New York City.

43

THE SECONDARY MARKET

The secondary market, or aftersale market, is where investors go to sell their municipal bonds, or to purchase other investors' existing (used) bonds. When purchasing a bond in the primary market (new issue market), money is, in effect, being channeled to the issuing municipality. However this is not the case when buying bonds in the secondary market, where new money is not being raised by the municipality. Rather, one investor with money to invest is providing liquidity to another investor who wishes to convert his/her bonds to cash.

The municipal bond market maintains no formal exchange for the trading—buying and selling—of existing municipal bonds. Municipal bonds are thus traded in an informal market made up of a large group of brokerage houses, banks, and municipal boutiques, which are relatively small firms specializing in municipal bonds, widely dispersed throughout the country. A secondary market in municipal securities is made available with the help of the Blue List (see Key 44), various information systems, such as Bloomberg and Kennybase, brokers' brokers (see Key 45), and the ubiquitous telephone. Municipal bond dealers continually purchase municipal securities from those wishing to sell and subsequently resell these seasoned issues to interested buyers.

An example of a secondary market transaction follows.

An investor wishing to sell $100,000 face value of California general obligation bonds calls municipal bond Dealer A, a brokerage house, for instance, to solicit a "bid," a price that the dealer is willing to pay for the bonds. If pleased with the price quoted, the investor will sell the bonds to Dealer A ("hit the bid"). Now that

Dealer A owns $100,000 face value California bonds, the following can occur:

- Dealer A can add these bonds to the brokerage house's inventory—bonds owned and held by the firm's traders (see Key 40). These bonds can then be actively marketed by the firm's salespeople to the existing client base at a markup from cost, or held indefinitely in anticipation of future price appreciation. In the case of the latter, the dealer hopes to sell the bonds sometime in the near future at an even higher price.

- At the same time, Dealer A may choose to advertise these California bonds either in the Blue List, through the various information services, such as Bond Track and Bloomberg, etc., or through a broker's broker. Other dealer firms noticing the advertisement and having a need to fill one of their customer's orders, may call Dealer A to purchase the bonds. When selling to another dealer ("to the street"), Dealer A may choose to give a price break, or a concession. This amounts to a wholesale price offered to the dealer community. However, in this competitive environment, large institutional customers may demand this advantageous pricing as well.

- If Dealer A is unsuccessful in selling these California bonds through the strategies mentioned above, on the offered side, then, as a last resort he/she can initiate an auction process. The auction, normally conducted through a broker's broker, will be discussed in Key 45. In this scenario, Dealer A is, in essence, throwing up his/her hands and saying to the dealer community, "OK, if you don't like these bonds at my advertised price, then at what price do you want to buy them?"

44

THE BLUE LIST

The Blue List, published daily by Standard & Poor's, is a current listing of municipal bonds that bond dealers own and choose to advertise. It is similar to the real estate classified section of the Sunday newspaper, except that it is not normally distributed to the general public. However, investors wishing to subscribe may do so for a substantial annual fee.

The municipal bonds listed in the Blue List are broken down alphabetically by state. In addition, they are categorized by various investment characteristics, including: prefunded bonds (see Key 22), notes (see Key 27), alternative minimum tax (AMT) bonds (see Key 5), and zero coupon bonds (see Key 24).

The Blue List is a municipal bond trader's and salesman's bible, providing invaluable information regarding the prices and yields on a wide variety of municipal securities. Bonds listed in the Blue List can be purchased by calling the appropriate advertising dealer.

How to Read the Blue List.

EXAMPLE:

Amount	Security	Rate	Maturity	Yield or Price	Offered By
100	N.Y. St.	6.00	11/15/06	5.95	Bk. Of N.Y.
	CA 96 @ 102.5:01 @100				

This listing, taken out of the Blue List, can be read as follows:

$100,000 face value (principal) of bonds issued by New York State, with a coupon rate (stated interest rate) of 6 percent and a maturity date of November 1, 2006, are offered at a yield to maturity of 5.95 percent by the Bank of New York. The bonds are callable in 1996 at a price of 102.50 ($1,025 per $1,000 bond), and can be continually called at a declining value until 2001, when on that date and thereafter they can be called at par ($1,000 per $1,000 bond).

The Blue List does not include in its listings bond CUSIP (identification) numbers or the dealer's concession (price break offered to dealers). This information must be obtained from calling the advertising dealer. Since the Blue List is not an on-line (computer-generated) service, many listings are stale, that is, previously sold and never removed from the listings, price or yield change not reflected in the listing, etc. Therefore, it is important for traders and salespeople to call the offering dealers to check the accuracy of the listing (freshen up the offering). In addition, the Blue List does not publish bond ratings. Ratings can be found by accessing computer-based information systems, such as Kennybase or Bloomberg, looking in rating books published by Moody's and Standard & Poor's, or for the most up-to-date and accurate information, calling the rating agencies directly.

While the continued proliferation of computer-based information systems threatens the very survival of the Blue List, for the time being, it is doing just fine. Virtually all traders and salespeople involved with municipal bonds faithfully use the Blue List on a daily basis.

45

BROKERS' BROKERS

Individual investors have little or no reason to interact with a municipal bond broker's broker—in reality a dealer's broker—since these brokers do not maintain inventories, deal with the general public, or trade for their own accounts. Their job is to facilitate trading among the municipal bond dealer community. As in any industry, the broker's purpose is to match buyers with sellers. When looking to buy a house, for example, many potential homebuyers contact real estate agents (brokers) whose knowledge of the homes available in a desired area enable them to reap a commission for their efforts. Similarly, a bond broker's knowledge of the market and its participants, enables him/her to act as a middleman, providing a service for a commission. It is important to remember that the primary difference between a dealer and a broker is that a broker does not maintain inventories of bonds.

Bid-Wanted Process. An important function that most municipal brokers provide is that of an auctioneer conducting what the market terms a *bid-wanted process*. When a dealer firm is seeking to sell a bond on behalf of a customer and has no desire to place the bond into its own inventory, or cannot find a customer for the particular bond, or wants to sell a bond in inventory that no one seems to want to buy at the advertised price that may appear in the Blue List, the firm can approach a broker's broker with a request to go bid-wanted. With a bid-wanted, an auction process is initiated as follows:

1. The firm (Dealer A) wishing to sell a bond, contacts its favorite broker, stating that it wishes to go bid-wanted.

2. The broker then circulates the full description of the bond, via computer terminals, to all participating bond dealers throughout the country. Each of the dealers interested in buying the bond then submits a bid to the broker.
3. The broker then compiles all the bids and presents the high bid (lowest yield and highest price) minus the broker's commission to Dealer A.
4. Dealer A decides, possibly in conjunction with its customer, whether it wishes to sell the bond at the price presented by the broker (hit the bid).
5. If Dealer A decides to hit the bid, the broker then buys the bond from Dealer A and subsequently sells it to Dealer B, the high bidder.

Two of the most utilized municipal brokers' brokers are J. J. Kenny and Chapdalaine, both of which possess a wire service (Kenny Wire, and C Wire), which on an average day, list hundreds of bid wanteds. These two firms are the brokers of choice for dealers seeking to sell garden variety municipal bonds. Other municipal bond brokers include, but are not limited to, Cantor Fitzgerald, Tullet of Tokyo, E.M.R., Titus and Donnelly, and R.W. Smith. Each of these brokers may specialize in a specific type of bond, geographic area, or maturity range. For example, Titus and Donnelly does an excellent job handling New York issues, whereas Tullet specializes in large blocks of prerefunded bonds.

Although the general public cannot deal directly with one of these brokers, knowledge of how the broker system functions can give the investor a better insight into the operation of the municipal bond market.

46

RATING AGENCIES

Due to a lack of time, as well as limited financial sophistication on the part of investors, rating agencies are heavily relied upon to assess the credit quality of municipal bond issues. It is recommended, however, that investors conduct independent research prior to investing in tax-exempt securities.

Rating agencies give the municipal bond investor a basic grading system that compares the investment quality of various issuers, attempting to answer the fundamental question: Will the investor be repaid earned interest and principal in a timely fashion?

The two best known and utilized rating agencies are Moody's Investors Service, and Standard & Poor's, Inc. Fitch Investors Service, a third rating agency, is relied upon to a far lesser degree. Of the two primary rating agencies, Moody's is arguably the most conservative and reliable. However, Standard & Poor's (S&P) is considered more proficient in certain specialties of municipal finance, such as the rating of corporate-type municipal bonds (see Key 29, Variable-Rate Demand Bonds). Overall, both these firms do an adequate job of risk analysis and can be used interchangeably.

Moody's Long-Term Rating System. A discussion of Moody's rating system is as follows:

In descending order of quality, there are nine rating symbols: Aaa, Aa, A, Baa, Ba, B, Caa, Ca, C. When analysts at Moody's believe that bonds in a particular category possess the strongest investment attributes of that group a 1 is placed after the letter to denote this fact (AA1, A1, Baa1). Bonds rated Aaa and Caa and lower are never designated with the 1 symbol.

Aaa. Aaa bonds are of the highest quality, possessing the lowest degree of default risk; they are considered gilt-edged.

Aa. Aa bonds are considered of high quality; however, margins of protection against changes in the municipality's financial condition are weaker than with Aaa-rated bonds. This classification, coupled with Aaa, comprise what the market refers to as high-grade securities.

A. A-rated bonds are upper medium-grade quality, with the outlook for timely repayment of principal and interest currently adequate; however, it is felt that contingencies exist that could impair future repayment of the bonds.

Baa. Baa-rated bonds are medium-grade obligations possessing certain speculative elements. Prospects for timely repayment of principal and interest are adequate at present, but in the long term, protective factors may be lacking.

Ba. The future of bonds in this category is not well assured. Bonds in this category are considered to be somewhat speculative, with a minimal amount of protection against contingencies.

B. Bonds in this classification are not considered an acceptable investment due to much uncertainty regarding timely repayment of future interest and principal.

Caa. Bonds in this category involve issuers who may currently be experiencing financial difficulty. A very real danger exists in regard to timely repayment.

Ca. Bonds in this classification are highly speculative. A high probability exists that the bonds may be in default.

C. The chances of any bond in this category ever becoming investment grade is minimal. This is the bottom of the ratings classes.

Bonds classified Baa and better are considered by the market as investment grade securities. It is highly recommended that most investors purchase only these securities, as higher returns offered on more speculative bonds may not compensate for the increased risk of default. Only sophisticated investors with an abundance of information should even consider dealing in noninvestment grade bonds (see Key 25).

Moody's Short-Term Ratings. In addition to the bond ratings (long-term) discussed above, Moody's publishes a short-term grading system. Emphasis is placed on the issuer's cash flow and liquidity (cash on hand), rather than on long-term variables and trends, such as employment trends in the community and wealth levels. When rating short-term securities, the basic question that must be answered is: Will there be enough cash on hand in a year or two when the bonds mature to repay the investor?

A discussion of Moody's short-term grading system is as follows:

When rating short-term municipal securities, Moody's appoints MIG (Moody's Investment Grade) ratings from 1 to 4 based upon the issuer's creditworthiness, liquidity, cash flow, ability to access the financial markets for refinancing, and overall protection to the investor. Issues rated SG are considered speculative, and not of investment grade.

MIG1. Best short-term rating, indicating high liquidity, superior cash flow, and a high degree of accessibility to the capital markets.

MIG2. While evidencing good quality, margins of protection with MIG2 bonds are not as wide as with MIG1 paper.

MIG3. While quality is again currently favorable, access to the financial markets may be somewhat limited, and margins of protection may be small.

MIG4. With MIG4-rated securities, a significant degree of risk is present. While currently in satisfactory condition, bonds rated MIG4 contain elements that may lead to future problems.

SG. These securities are not considered investment grade, since margins of protection for the investor are wanting.

When rating variable-rate demand bonds (Key 29), Moody's denotes the short-term ratings as VMIG1-4, emphasizing that the liquidity is based on something other than a stated maturity, such as a tender to a third party.

The rating system should not be used as a way to gauge the attractiveness of a bond. Investors must supplement the information obtained from the rating agencies with their own research and common sense. This may be a difficult objective to achieve, since, in reality, due to a lack of time, a degree of laziness, and a historically good job done by the rating bureau, investors have become overly reliant on the rating agencies.

Standard & Poor's maintains a rating system similar to Moody's.

47

BOND INSURANCE

For municipal bond investors seeking some added security, bond insurance may be just what the doctor ordered. The six municipal insurers, whose claim-paying abilities—the ability to pay interest and principal to bondholders in the event of a default on the part of the issuer—are rated AAA, are AMBAC Indemnity Corporation (AMBAC), Capital Guarantee Insurance Company (CAP Guarantee), Capital Markets Assurance Corporation (Cap Mac), Financial Guarantee Insurance Company (FGIC), Financial Security Assurance Incorporated (FSA), and Municipal Bond Investors Assurance (MBIA). Bonds offered with insurance from any other carrier should be researched extensively.

Municipal insurers are contacted by bond underwriters (see Key 40) at the time of issuance who request, in exchange for the payment of a premium, the insurance company's guarantee of timely payment of interest and principal. The bond underwriter is betting that the cost of insurance will be more than offset by the ability to sell these enhanced securities at a higher price. Traders (see Key 40) who maintain a position of uninsured bonds (secondary market) may contact the insurer as well, to insure these bonds that are already outstanding. The trader is again betting that the cost of this secondary market insurance will be outweighed by a higher price commanded for the bonds.

Many municipal investors have had an ongoing love affair with insured municipal bonds. By giving up a relatively small amount of return, such as 10 to 60 basis points, the investor has the comfort of knowing that the insurer, independent of the rating agencies, has conducted an in-depth credit analysis of the issuing municipality.

Once the analysis is completed, and the insurer commits to the underwriting, all financial resources at the insurance company's disposal are pledged to repay the investor in the event the municipality defaults on its debt.

Unlike the rating agency (see Key 46), insurers are putting their money where their mouth is, realizing that a miscalculation could cause a severe financial hardship for the firm, as claims are paid. Municipal insurers normally target bonds that are rated Baa to A. Bonds rated below Baa may be deemed too risky to insure, whereas insurance may also be unnecessary for bonds rated higher than A. Investors normally have a huge appetite for these securities based on their own merits.

How Strong Is the Insurers' Guarantee? The insurance placed on a bond is only as secure as the insurance company itself. The claims-paying ability of these muni-bond insurers is a function of its capital base (policyholder surplus plus contingency reserves), depression lines of credit (the ability to borrow from banks), and income generated from vast holdings of investment securities. In addition, these insurers often engage in reinsurance arrangements, selling off a portion of their claim liabilities to other insurers.

There are different schools of thought regarding the benefits of bond insurance. Two extreme arguments are as follows:

Anti-insurance. A primary reason that municipal insurers have maintained such a high degree of creditworthiness is due to the fact that there have been relatively few municipal bankruptcies. Therefore, municipal insurance is most often superfluous, giving investors an unneeded sense of security on bonds that have an incredible track record on principal and interest repayment. Furthermore, the infrequency of paying out claims has enabled these firms to build generous capital bases and investment portfolios. In the unlikely event that a string of significant municipal bankruptcies prevailed, the creditworthiness of the insurance companies would indeed suffer at a time when you need them the most. While the rating agencies give AAA ratings to the insurers listed above, the market views insured AAA bonds as lower credit quality than bonds achieving AAA on their own.

Pro-insurance. Those municipal insurers rated AAA by Moody's and/or Standard & Poor's have truly earned their gilt-edged rating, maintaining more than sufficient levels of capital to guard against a large number of municipal bankruptcies. Moreover, municipal insurers have had a stellar record of claims payments, albeit relatively few claims, in recent history. It is important to note that, in the event of a municipal default on a bond covered by insurance, the insurer is not required to pay off the principal immediately, but must service the periodic interest payments up until the maturity date, at which time principal must be paid, assuming the municipality has not by this time remedied its financial problems. Unlike AAA uninsured bonds, where a municipality receives an AAA rating based on its own merits, insured municipal bonds have double-barrel repayment capabilities. They retain as the primary source of repayment the financial resources of the issuer. If not sufficient, the insurance company's guarantee would kick in.

The true value of bond insurance probably lies somewhere between the two arguments mentioned above. Insurance, while not a panacea to one's credit concerns, can definitely be an integral part of effective portfolio management.

48

MANAGING A MUNICIPAL BOND PORTFOLIO

Successfully investing in municipal bonds entails far more than arbitrarily purchasing a series of tax-exempt bonds; a good deal of time must be expended managing the portfolio. This involves the understanding of the economy, the credit risks associated with municipal bonds, interest rate risk, and good old common sense.

Managing Credit Risk. Managing credit risk involves using all available resources to reduce the risk of financial loss arising out of deteriorating financial conditions of municipal issuers. Declining credit quality can lead to a precipitous drop in the market value of a security, and ultimately in bond default. Following is a discussion of some viable strategies in attempting to mitigate credit risk.

Due to a lack of both time and sophistication, investors often tend to rely heavily on the ratings assigned by Moody's and Standard & Poor's. These rating agencies provide a convenient gradation system to assist the investor in choosing among issuers. While normally an excellent place to begin one's analysis, an overreliance on bond ratings can be extremely risky. The rating agencies do not perform audits, nor do they state that all information received and published is accurate (see Key 46). Investors must, therefore, review as much research as possible, including rating agency research reports and reports written by brokerage houses and banks, in addition to thoroughly reading the official statement (Key 55).

Insured municipal bonds (see Key 47) may be worth considering, especially for those with little confidence in

146

their own credit review skills. Having an AAA insured bond gives the investor a degree of comfort in addition to the general obligation pledge or revenue flows of the underlying issue. The marginal amount of return given up to pay for this insurance may prove very worthwhile in the event of an unexpected bankruptcy.

Prerefunded bonds, or preres (see Key 22) should undoubtedly be included in the municipal bond portfolio of any investor desiring the highest credit quality. These U.S. government-backed bonds yield only slightly less than most medium-grade securities, and are thus a no-lose proposition. The greater percentage of preres in the portfolio, the better the investor should sleep at night.

In managing a municipal portfolio, the need for diversification cannot be overemphasized. No more than a certain percentage of the portfolio should be invested in any one issue or issuer. A guideline of no more than 5 to 10 percent in any one issue name may prove helpful. By purchasing greater numbers of different issues, the investor is, in effect, diversifying away a portion of the credit risk. Investors should attempt to diversify geographically as well. However, when purchasing bonds issued by municipalities outside one's state of residency, one is forced to pay state and local taxes on the income generated from those bonds. The credit quality benefits derived from spreading the risk across state lines may far outweigh this financial penalty.

Managing Interest Rate Risk. Rising interest rates can quietly erode the value of a municipal bond portfolio. The longer the average maturity of the portfolio, the greater its price volatility. At the same time, by investing in longer maturities, the investor is normally rewarded with a higher yield to maturity (upward sloping yield curve). What we have is a tug-of-war between shorter, safer, and lower-yielding short-term bonds, and the longer, more volatile, and higher-yielding bonds. The successful manager must balance these two issues, attempting to maximize the portfolio's return and at the same time protect the portfolio against rising interest rates.

If an investor somehow possesses a crystal ball, and is able to forecast which way interest rates are going to move, the strategy is simple: If interest rates are presumed to rise, then buy very short-term bonds; if forecasted to fall, extend the maturity horizon. However, without this crystal ball, consistently and successfully predicting interest rate movements is a virtual impossibility for the beginner investor. Even professional Wall Street economists have a difficult time continually predicting which way interest rates are going to move. For every distinguished economist forecasting higher interest rates, there is another with equally impressive credentials, predicting a drop in rates. Therefore, it is important to consider the following strategies to mitigate this interest rate risk:

- *Ladder approach.* Investors should stagger the bond's maturities over a certain time horizon. For example, an investor with $200,000 to invest can purchase eight blocks of $25,000 maturing in two through ten years. Each year $25,000 matures, and can thus be reinvested at the prevailing interest rates. A more aggressive investor may choose to increase the average life of the portfolio, while a more conservative investor may choose to decrease the overall maturity lengths, that is, buy four blocks of $50,000 maturing from one to four years.

- *Barbell approach.* Investors should invest roughly half of the portfolio's funds long-term, and the remaining half short-term. For example, a $200,000 portfolio can be broken down as follows: $100,000 maturing in one year, and the remaining $100,000 maturing in 20 years. The portfolio return is a blended average of the yield to maturity of the higher-yielding 20-year bonds, presuming an upward sloping yield curve, and the lower-yielding, yet less volatile, one-year bonds. If interest rates were to rise, the short-term bonds could be reinvested at higher yields. If interest rates were to fall, the long-term bonds would increase in value, while the short-term bonds would be rolled over at the lower prevailing rates.

Both these strategies are designed to hedge the portfolio against interest movements, and may preclude the portfolio manager from hitting a home run—that is, correctly calling the interest movement and exploiting it with the correct maturity structure. The ladder strategy is arguably the simplest and most effective approach; it can be a tremendous help in one's portfolio management.

Strategies to Enhance Portfolio Returns. Following are some strategies the investor can employ.

- *Odd lots*. For buy-and-hold investors, purchasing odd lots—blocks of $20,000 or less—may enable the investor to net a higher yield to maturity. This higher return compensates for the nuisance of increased bookkeeping, as well as the diminished liquidity; odd lots are difficult to sell in the aftersale market.

- *Alternative minimum tax bonds*. For those investors who are not currently subject, nor expect to be subject to the alternative minimum tax, AMT bonds are a great find. They offer a higher return than conventional non-AMT bonds (see Key 5). They are, however, less marketable than conventional non-AMT bonds.

- *Private placements*. Municipalities wishing to borrow a relatively small sum of money may wish to avoid the high fixed costs associated with a full-blown underwriting, and thus may contact a bank or investment house, to arrange an informal loan. A qualified investor, purchasing a private placement—in effect informally lending funds to the municipality—receives no official statement (limited amount of investment information), and forgoes a good deal of liquidity. The investor should thus be compensated in the form of a significantly higher yield to maturity when purchasing private placements. Only sophisticated investors should consider buying these issues.

49

TAX-EXEMPT INVESTMENT MANAGEMENT

Tax-exempt investment management may provide an alternative to investing in a municipal bond mutual fund, or dedicating the time to build one's own municipal bond portfolio. With an investment management account, the investor's funds are professionally handled by either an investment firm or a bank, as part of an overall balanced portfolio in which stocks and bonds are commingled within the same portfolio or as a stand-alone municipal bond portfolio.

Advantages of a Managed Account.

1. It enables individuals to be free from day-to-day investment decisions, allowing them to enjoy their retirement or wealth, travel the world, or enjoy various hobbies, other than financial.
2. It offers more flexibility to the investor than a municipal mutual fund. The investor, in this scenario, can give input to the money manager regarding what types of bonds to purchase and the average maturity of the portfolio, as well as the overall degree of risk to be assumed.
3. Investment portfolios are normally monitored for changes in their credit quality. An astute money manager can hopefully detect a deteriorating situation promptly and act upon the information obtained to minimize the financial loss to the investor.
4. Dealing with a reputable investment manager can protect the investor from unscrupulous bond brokers looking to sell marginal quality bonds at

inflated prices. While some complain that the fees charged by many money managers are prohibitive, the devil one knows may turn out to be better than the devil one does not know.

5. While it may be nearly impossible to consistently call market movements correctly, some investment managers are better than others. Finding this diamond in the rough may enable the investor to realize capital gains in addition to tax-free income. While past success does not necessarily predict future performance, it is nonetheless important to ask prospective investment managers for their portfolio returns over a prior period of time—five years is not an unreasonable accountability period.

Disadvantages of a Managed Account.

1. The fees charged for a managed municipal account are often quite high. They may range from 25 basis points (¼ of 1 percent) to those in excess of 100 basis points (1 percent), based upon the sum invested. For example, an investor who pays a municipal money manager $1,000,000 can be charged anywhere from $2,500 to over $10,000. It may be difficult for an investment manager to justify this cost structure. Investors who have both the time and financial background may choose to create their own portfolios. Many investors find municipals no mystery and with a little study and effort can master municipal bond investing.

2. While investment managers tout their uncanny ability to monitor the portfolio for changing credit quality and act *ahead* of the overall market, the sad truth is that many tend to react *after* the fact. For example, many managers tend to sell bonds following a downgrade by a rating agency, rather than before. The result is no value added in this area.

3. Investors who are enamored with the idea of their bond portfolio being professionally managed may find that, to their chagrin, their level of assets precludes them from being considered for this service.

151

Investment managers normally require a minimum portfolio size, often ranging from $250,000 to $1,000,000.

4. While paying someone to manage your wealth may appear attractive and may lessen your own day-to-day burdens, it is nonetheless practically impossible to abdicate one's financial responsibilities. An incompetent money manager can go a long way in destroying the wealth that has been created or accrued to you over the years. Before entrusting your funds to any individual or firm, do your homework with an extensive background check.

50

THE SINKING FUND

A sinking fund provision, quite common in the issuance of industrial bonds and utility debt, is employed by investment bankers in the muni-bond world as well. A sinking fund requires the issuer to redeem an established amount of bonds in specific years prior to the bonds' stated maturity. Funds are set aside and then given to a trustee who is empowered to conduct a lottery for the purpose of calling the required number of bonds. In virtually all cases, bonds called from a sinking fund are redeemed at par, as opposed to total calls that are often at a premium-to-face value, such as 102, 101, etc.

In the municipal bond market, sinking funds are normally utilized with term bonds. (A term bond is among the longest maturities of a new issue, and normally makes up the bulk of the bonds that comprise the issue.) Five to ten years before the bond's maturity date, the issuer begins to call a portion of the outstanding term bonds every year until the bond matures. In effect, sinking funds shorten the bond's average life, as a fixed number of bonds are redeemed at par in each of the designated years. Investors have their funds returned to them more quickly than would be the case with similar bonds that contain no sinking fund provisions; consequently, the issuer gets to spread the payments over several years rather than paying all at once on the maturity date.

Advantages of Sinking Funds.

- Sinking fund bonds can be viewed as a defensive investment vehicle because, in a rising interest rate environment, investors receive a portion of their funds prior to maturity, enabling them to reinvest these funds at theoretically higher interest rates. As mentioned above, the sinking fund effectively shortens the bond's average maturity, or duration.

- The sinking fund allows the issuer an orderly repayment of debt over an extended period of time, leaving less to be repaid on the bond's maturity date. Invariably, this enhances the issuer's overall level of liquidity during the life of the issue.

Disadvantages of Sinking Funds.

- In a rallying bond market—a period of falling rates—sinking funds return to investors a portion of their funds that must now be reinvested at theoretically lower interest rates. Having a percentage of one's bonds called in prior to maturity effectively shortens the bond's average maturity. This makes it less volatile and, if compared to a comparable bond with no sinking fund, less likely to increase in value during a rallying municipal bond market.
- When purchasing a bond at a premium, a sinking fund call—as with any call prior to maturity—can be extremely dangerous, since it can significantly reduce the overall return. When a broker quotes a yield to maturity, there is an implicit assumption that the bond's redemption occurs on the maturity date. When dealing with a bond purchased above par, a sinking fund call prior to the stated maturity date will always result in a lower yield than quoted, and even possibly a significant loss. Whenever buying these premium issues, it is essential that the broker disclose whether any sinking funds are operative, and, if so, what the yield would be to each of the sinking fund dates.

In Wall Street jargon, the selling of bonds in the new sale market can be referred to as *floating* a bond issue. The *sinking* fund thus derives its name from this relationship. By understanding this concept, the investor can best utilize it in effective portfolio management and avoid the pitfall of being "sunk" at the wrong time!

51

SWAPS

A municipal bond swap involves the sale of a currently held bond and the simultaneous purchase of another bond to achieve a desired goal. This may involve creating a tax loss, changing the portfolio's maturity structure or credit characteristics, or exploiting a market anomaly. It is important for the investor to distinguish between swaps that actually improve one's financial position, and those with little economic merit, designed primarily to increase trading activity and ultimately improve the bond salesman's financial position.

Types of Swaps.

Tax-related swaps. Following a period of rising interest rates, investors may find bonds within their portfolio with significant paper losses. A technique used by investors to realize these tax losses, either to offset a current capital gain or to carry forward to a future year, is the tax swap.

A tax swap involves selling the underwater bond—the bond that presently has less value than the investor paid for it—thus booking the tax loss and at the same time purchasing new bonds that are materially different from the ones sold.

To be deemed a legitimate tax swap, the Internal Revenue Service requires that the newly purchased bonds be different from the ones sold in two of the three basic characteristics: issuer, rate, maturity.

For example, an investor selling a New York State, 7.00 percent Coupon Rate, Maturing July 1, 2007, could then purchase a New York State, 5.00 percent Coupon Rate, maturing July 1, 2000, to consummate a legal swap (both the coupon rate and maturity date differ). A purchase of a New York State, 7.00 percent Coupon Rate, Maturing July 1, 2005, however, would not be acceptable by the IRS, since the bonds sold and purchased only differ in their maturity dates.

Swaps that alter the portfolio's maturity structure. A bond swap may be initiated by an investor who wishes to either shorten or lengthen the portfolio's average maturity. In a market with the conventional upward sloping yield curve, in which longer maturities pay a higher yield (see Key 9), an investor with a sudden need to increase income can sell bonds with shorter maturities and replace them with higher-yielding long bonds. Conversely, investors with the ability to live on less income, looking to protect their capital from interest rate risk, can sell their longer maturity bonds and instead purchase less volatile, albeit lower-yielding short-term securities. Bonds with longer maturities fall in price more as interest rates increase than shorter maturities, all things being equal.

Swaps that alter the portfolio's credit characteristics. A bond swap can be implemented as well by investors either wishing to upgrade the quality of their portfolio, or desiring to increase their income. By selling lower quality bonds and replacing them with better rated securities, the investor will decrease the portfolios risk at the expense of lower income.

By replacing higher quality bonds with less dependable credits, investors seeking increased income can achieve their goals although lowering the overall credit strength of the portfolios.

Swaps initiated to exploit a market anomaly. Due to a shortage of certain kinds of municipal bonds (such as bonds issued by municipalities of a specific state or bonds maturing in a given year), market participants in desperate need of these bonds may be willing to pay a premium to capture this rare commodity. Investors possessing these bonds may choose to sell them at a scarcity-induced inflated price, replacing them with other higher-yielding securities.

For example, if a shortage of New York State bonds developed, Florida residents owning New York securities—

a Florida resident receives no added benefit from owning New York State bonds—could sell their bonds at a price reflecting their scarcity value and replace them with bonds issued by another state with an abundance of supply and consequently lower prices and higher yields. Similarly, a lack of two-year bonds may force certain market participants desperate for this maturity to pay inflated prices. Investors with an abundance of this maturity can again exploit this situation, swapping their two-year bonds for bonds of other maturities in more abundant supply.

A large municipal portfolio is often a tempting target for a municipal salesperson looking to generate added sales commissions. If there is no convincing reason to engage in a swap, don't!

52

THE SAFEKEEPING OF MUNICIPAL BONDS

Since the vast majority of bonds issued today are in book-entry form (see Key 17), the safekeeping of these bonds takes on increased importance. The question arises whether investors are best served by opening up comprehensive accounts at commercial banks, keeping their bonds at a major brokerage house, safekeeping them at a regional firm, or having a municipal boutique, which is a relatively small firm dealing primarily in tax-exempt bonds, hold the investors' securities?

Bank custody account. This is the most costly of the various alternatives. It is primarily for high net worth customers, since the high minimum charges may prove prohibitive for the small investor. Some banks for example, look for minimum assets of $250,000 with $1,000 the minimum holding (custody) fee. With bank custody accounts, customer assets are normally segregated from those of the bank. In the event of a bankruptcy on the part of the bank, creditors would have no claim on the assets of the bondholders. In addition, insurance coverage is generally taken by the bank as a protection against fraud and theft. Prior to signing a custody agreement, the investor may wish to verify that these safeguards are indeed in place. Some banks may provide the customer with a comfort letter to attest to this protection.

Banks that have municipal bond dealerships may also offer holding accounts at a marginal charge, or, in some cases, gratis for those bonds purchased from the bank. For those not desiring a full-blown custody account, and who buy bonds primarily from that bank, these *no-frills* accounts may be a perfect compromise.

It is important to note that securities held by a bank are not insured by the Federal Deposit Insurance Corporation (FDIC); the FDIC insures commercial bank deposits up to $100,0000. Nor does the bank guarantee the securities against municipal bankruptcies.

Safekeeping at a major brokerage house. With a few notable exceptions, such as Drexel Burnham, major brokerage houses have normally weathered the ups and downs of Wall Street business cycles. However, it is still of the utmost importance to understand the risks associated with safekeeping bonds at a brokerage house. Does the firm maintain adequate insurance coverage against various contingencies, such as theft? In the case of bankruptcy, what protection is afforded the customer? Securities Investor Protection Corporation (SIPC), for example, was established by Congress to protect customers from the failure of brokerage firms. Brokerage houses are normally required to join the SIPC, which insures securities and cash in the customer's account up to a specific amount.

Safekeeping at a regional brokerage house. Since less is probably known about the financial health of these smaller, less publicized firms, learning about the firm's insurance protection and its capitalization is even more important than in the case of these major brokerage houses. If the firm were to suffer major trading losses, for example, is there a sufficient cash cushion to keep the firm afloat?

Safekeeping at a municipal boutique. These relatively small houses specializing in tax-exempt securities range from well-capitalized, financially sound elite institutions to fly-by-night firms looking to defraud unsuspecting investors. It is imperative that the investor receives adequate responses to all the questions posed above, in addition to learning all that is known about the firm in question. Agencies such as the Securities and Exchange Commission (SEC), Municipal Securities Rulemaking Board (MSRB), and National Association of Security Dealers (NASD) may prove helpful in obtaining this important information.

53

THE THREE DEBACLES: NEW YORK CITY, WASHINGTON PUBLIC POWER SUPPLY SYSTEM (WPPSS), AND ORANGE COUNTY, CALIFORNIA

What do New York City, Washington Public Power Supply System (WPPSS), and Orange County, California, have in common? Their financial problems and ultimate defaults have changed the municipal landscape forever! Municipal bonds will never be viewed the same way again.

New York City. In November 1975 chronic budgetary abuses, overly optimistic forecasting of revenues, capitulating to the union's relentless salary and benefit demands, and exorbitant permanent short-term borrowings—a large-scale borrowing from Peter to pay Paul scheme—on the part of New York City came to a head. It culminated in a near financial collapse and default on over $2.5 billion of notes, a short-term debt.

New York State, sensing a financial disaster and potential default, demanded major fiscal changes before it would lend a helping hand. A major restructuring and consolidation of the city's government and municipal work force, including the elimination of jobs and a freeze on additional hiring, a ceiling on both the fiscal (yearly) and capital budgets, and an increase in university and transit payments by city residents, were among the many draconian measures demanded. The state established the Municipal Assistance Corporation (MAC) to help implement these changes, in an attempt to improve the overall economic condition of the city.

As far as the financial markets were concerned, this was too little too late; investor confidence was shattered! Noteholders who presented their IOUs (general obligation notes) for collection were instead given ten-year bonds backed by the newly formed Municipal Assistance Corporation (MAC). While these bonds offered the investor a hefty 8 percent tax-free interest rate, they nonetheless provided little help to those who needed their money at that moment, to pay for a house or college, for instance.

New York City appealed to Washington, D.C., for a federal bailout. The now infamous newspaper headline "Ford to New York: Go to Hell!" was the initial response. However, after submitting to a laundry list of fiscal demands, New York City was eventually granted federal relief.

To once again issue bonds through the public markets, New York City was forced to comply with federal and state demands, virtually handing over control of its financial affairs to a Financial Control Board. This board had complete control of the city's financial affairs—budgetary process, specific expenditures—for an extended period. While still in existence today solely in an advisory role, the Financial Control Board is authorized to spring back into action if a repeat of the fiscal follies of the 1970s reemerges, that is, if the city is unable to balance its budget.

To this day, more than two decades following the fateful default in 1975, New York City is still being penalized by the capital markets. A dichotomy exists, as some investors, many of whom were "burned" by New York City in the past, refuse to buy any New York City obligations at any price or yield. Others find the relative attractiveness of the penalty-driven higher yields more than sufficient to purchase an obligation issued by the "greatest city in the world."

Incidentally, the job of municipal analyst grew in scope and importance following the New York City crisis. Municipal bond firms, which had in the past generally neglected to employ in-house analysts, responded by setting up extensive research and analysis departments. General obligation bonds, considered prior to this disaster to be virtually risk free, now demanded a long, hard look.

Washington Public Power Supply System (WPPSS). In late 1983 the unimaginable happened when the Washington Public Power Supply System (WPPSS), the nation's largest issuer of tax-exempt debt, defaulted on $2.25 *billion* worth of bonds.

The Washington Public Power Supply System, a joint action agency of Washington State (see Key 38), was established in the late 1950s to supply energy to the Northwest region of the United States. In response to predictions of continued growth forecast for the region, WPPSS's mandate was to supplement the hydroelectric power production by supplying nuclear power to energy users. Through the 1970s and early 1980s massive amounts of bonds were floated by WPPSS to finance the construction of five nuclear generating plants, projects 1, 2, 3, 4, and 5. From the outset, innumerable problems plagued these projects. They included:

- Protracted construction delays resulted in severe cost overruns. A 1976 projected total cost estimate of a little over $7 billion was revised in 1981 to a staggering $20-odd billion.
- America's love affair with nuclear power seemed to be waning as a prolonged oil shortage ended.
- Demand for power in the Northwest fell short of estimates.
- The overall viability of the projects seemed to be in question due in part to the above-mentioned factors. It seemed as if the plants would never be able to produce power economically and efficiently.

While all five projects were plagued by similar problems, only the now infamous projects 4 and 5 actually defaulted on their debt payments. Bonds issued for projects 1, 2, and 3 were ultimately obligations of the Bonneville Power Administration (BPA), a seller of power in the Northwest. BPA was required to increase customer rates to a level necessary to pay interest and principal—in effect billing the customers—whether or not these projects were ever built and/or operating. This "fall back" to the Bonneville Power's creditworthiness spared holders of WPPSS's projects 1, 2, and 3 a great deal of grief, not to mention a great deal of money, more than $6 billion in bonds were outstanding for these three projects. Bondholders of projects 4 and 5 however, were not so lucky.

Projects 4 and 5. Rather than relying on Bonneville Power, projects 4 and 5 were backed by 88 utilities in Washington, Oregon, and Idaho, which entered into take-or-pay contracts. As you may remember from Key 38 (Public Power Bonds), take-or-pay contracts should protect bondholders from just this type of contingency. Regardless of whether the plants were built or not, the take-or-pay provision required the utility participants to set sufficient rates from their existing power plants to adequately meet the total cost of the projects, including the servicing of debt. In January 1982, discussions about the possible mothballing of projects 4 and 5 culminated in outright termination of these projects. Bondholders of WPPSS's projects 4 and 5 drew some measure of comfort from the take-or-pay contracts shifting the financial burden to the ratepayers of the Northwest. Unfortunately, to the chagrin of bondholders, the unthinkable happened: Washington, Oregon, and Idaho courts declared the take-or-pay contract void, arguing that the 88 utilities did not possess the legal right to enter into these agreements in the first place. This decree left bondholders holding nothing but the bag!

What followed was a massive fraud trial with more than 20,000 bondholders suing everyone involved: engineers, dealers, rating agencies, and more. Bondholders ultimately settled, hoping to receive less than 50 cents on the dollar.

Since WPPSS, analysts and investors seemed determined not to let past mistakes and oversights repeat themselves. The default changed revenue bond analysis to the same astounding degree that the New York City default altered the analysis of general obligation bonds. When analyzing revenue bonds, greater attention is now paid to matters such as contract law, forecasted project costs, and construction costs and delays.

Orange County, California. The 1970s had the New York City debacle, and the 1980s had WPPSS. The 1990s, not to be outdone, brought the Orange County bankruptcy. The bankruptcy filing and the ensuing events sent shock waves through the municipal market.

On the afternoon of November 24, 1994, rumors began to circulate through Wall Street trading rooms that Orange County had suffered exorbitant losses on its investment portfolio. Before long, it was confirmed. Due primarily to extensive leveraging—the borrowing of additional funds using the portfolio as collateral, then purchasing even more securities—of its fixed-income portfolio and, to a lesser degree, losses on derivatives, Orange County had suffered close to a $2 billion portfolio loss. Soon after, to the chagrin of the municipal bond market, Orange County had filed for Chapter 9 bankruptcy protection. The filing, while not unprecedented—in 1991 Bridgeport, Connecticut, became the first major city to file for bankruptcy protection—nonetheless dealt a devastating blow to the entire municipal market. When times get real tough, could a municipality in trouble just declare bankruptcy and repudiate its debt, and, in effect, walk away from its general obligation pledge? Both Moody's and Standard & Poor's suffered great embarrassment when it was revealed that they were totally unaware of the blatantly fraudulent investment activities conducted by Orange County's now infamous ex-treasurer, Robert Citron. Prior to these revelations, they had rated Orange County as extremely creditworthy. The municipal market came to a virtual standstill, wondering what the future would bring, especially for holders of Orange County securities. It seemed that no one, not

Orange County residents nor the governor of California, nor the federal government wanted to promptly put this debacle to rest.

On June 27, 1995, Orange County residents voted down a one-half cent increase in the county's sales tax, eliminating a significant revenue stream that could be used in repaying debtholders. A key part of the municipality's overall rescue package was now gone, and the dreadful saga continued.

With a large amount ($800 million) of short-term notes (see Key 27) due for repayment in July and August of 1995, the market waited with bated breath to see what actions Orange County would take to appease debtholders. Due to the bankruptcy filing, the county was under no legal obligation to repay the notes when due. In typical fashion, Orange County, rather than paying off these notes, come hell or high water, as implied by the general obligation pledge, requested a year-long extension to June 1996. Noteholders, under threat of nonpayment (ever!), agreed to extend the notes' maturity dates. The extension of these notes was viewed by market participants as a technical *default*.

Finally, in September of the same year, the California State Legislature approved a recovery plan for Orange County, setting the way for the county to emerge from bankruptcy. Major features of the recovery plan include:

- diversion of moneys (close to $67 million annually) from the Orange County Transportation Agency (OCTA), the county solid waste system, and other special districts, to Orange County's general fund
- the establishment of a mechanism to seize county revenues for the benefit of debtholders, an intercept mechanism;
- the new revenues diverted to the county, and the intercept mechanism to allow the county to issue over $500 million in new bonds, the proceeds of which will be earmarked to pay off a good portion of the notes that now come due in June 1996; and

- the stipulation that, if the rescue package does not perform as planned, a state trustee wielding strong powers may be appointed.

Overall, it seems likely that most debtholders will eventually be repaid in full.

The Orange County bankruptcy is a tale of an incompetent and overzealous treasurer, and a wealthy county whose antitax stance, and unwillingness to do the right thing immediately, such as raise taxes and/or reduce expenditures, threatened the viability of the entire municipal bond market. Fortunately, however, almost one year after the market learned of the staggering investment losses, things have pretty much returned to normal. For many months, because of Orange County's actions, California municipalities had to sell their bonds at extremely high yields to compensate for the perceived risk. Today, once again, they can sell bonds at customary yields. The Orange County disaster, and the conduct thereafter, was viewed by the market as an isolated event. The municipal bond market, however, learned one very important lesson: The *willingness* of a municipality to repay its debt is every bit as important as its ability to repay its obligations.

54

REGULATION OF THE MUNICIPAL BOND MARKET

While there are numerous regulatory bodies supervising the municipal bond industry, the most prominent agency policing the industry is undoubtedly the Municipal Securities Rulemaking Board (MSRB). Created by Congress in the mid-1970s, the MSRB promulgates rules and regulations affecting both the dealer and broker community. It consists of 15 members equally divided among representatives of brokerage houses, bank dealers, and the investing public. The Municipal Securities Rulemaking Board is considered a self-regulated body financed by fees paid by those dealer firms being regulated. The Securities and Exchange Commission (SEC) oversees the day-to-day activities of the MSRB in addition to approving the regulations created by the board. A major responsibility of the MSRB is to protect municipal bond investors from unscrupulous market dealers and practices. To achieve this objective, the MSRB requires:

1. that there be investor suitability, in that any municipal investment sold to an investor must be *suitable* to that investor's current needs and objectives; for example, a Ca-rated municipal junk bond maturing in 20 years is probably not suitable for an unsophisticated octogenarian investor
2. that no false or deceptive advertising be undertaken by municipal security dealers; for example, a Baa bond should not be advertised as possessing outstanding credit quality, but should be described accurately as a medium-grade security

3. full disclosure of all relevant facts relating to the security in question, enabling the investor to make an educated decision regarding the potential purchase
4. that dealers never guarantee an investor against a market loss relating to a security purchased; a statement by a municipal salesperson such as "Buy this bond now, and if it decreases in value, my firm will reimburse you" would constitute a violation of MSRB regulations
5. that municipal securities be sold at *reasonable* prices, limiting the markup on securities to a fair spread over dealer cost.
6. that, following the purchase or sale of a municipal bond, a confirm must be sent on a timely basis to the customer (see Key 16)
7. that an official statement (prospectus) must be sent on a timely basis to any investor purchasing a municipal bond in the new issue (primary) market.

For any municipal bond investors who feel they have been wronged by a municipal dealer firm and are unable to settle the dispute amicably, the MSRB provides a forum for its resolution, namely, the *arbitration program*. The aggrieved investor goes before a panel of impartial arbitrators who render a binding decision regarding the complaint at hand; however, by pleading one's case before an arbitration panel, an investor normally gives up the right to settle the dispute in a court of law.

Other regulatory authorities involved in one way or another with the supervision of the municipal bond market include the National Association of Security Dealers (NASD), the Federal Deposit Insurance Company (FDIC), the Federal Reserve Bank (the Fed), Office of the Comptroller, the Internal Revenue Service (IRS), and the U.S. Treasury Department.

55

INFORMATION SOURCES

It is essential that the investor perform some degree of independent research prior to investing in a municipal bond. The ills associated with an overreliance on published ratings, such as Moody's and Standard & Poor's, have been articulated throughout this book and can sometimes have dire consequences. Information regarding the municipal bond market can be obtained from many sources, which include, but are not limited to the following:

- *The official statement* (*prospectus*)—a legal document prepared by the municipal issuer in conjunction with a financial advisor. It consists of extensive information about the municipality and the overall bond deal. This information includes a description of the municipal issuer, key demographic facts, the purpose of the bond issue, the security pledged to back the bonds, outstanding litigation, etc. Overall, the official statement is the forum in which the municipality discloses all relevant facts that are considered to be material, in other words, what a sensible investor should know prior to purchasing the bonds.
- *Research reports*—reports that are published by rating agencies, such as Moody's and Standard & Poor's, and brokerage houses.
- *The Bond Buyer*—a trade newspaper published daily, containing comprehensive information on the municipal and Treasury bond market, including upcoming primary market sales, relevant news stories, and yield information.
- *The Blue List* (see Key 44).

- *Materials and brochures*—material published by the Public Securities Association (PSA).

The above-mentioned materials can be obtained by calling your broker or writing to the appropriate party. In addition, there is much widely available information that can aid in successful municipal bond investing. Information regarding the economy, the overall bond market (fixed-income markets), as well as the municipal market can be obtained from:

- *The Wall Street Journal.* Each issue contains a *credit markets* column (*bond market*) with a special section devoted exclusively to municipal bonds. The *Journal* is required reading for any serious investor.
- *The New York Times.* This newspaper also publishes a daily credit markets column, but with no special section devoted to municipal bonds.
- *Barron's.* This weekly business publication provides valuable fixed-income investment advice.
- *Business Week*, *Forbes*, and *Fortune.* These and other financial magazines can prove helpful in broadening the investor's understanding of the business world and financial markets. They may also occasionally contain some valuable information on the municipal market.

The more information at an investor's fingertips, the better. Remember, one can never be too rich, too thin, or have too much financial information!

56

TAX REFORM AND THE FUTURE OF THE MUNICIPAL BOND MARKET

Following the Tax Reform Act of 1986, cries of the demise of the municipal bond market echoed through Wall Street. The act significantly reduced the volume of tax-exempt issuance, virtually eliminating total classifications of bonds. Furthermore, major buyers of municipal bonds—banks and insurance companies—lost various tax benefits associated with their purchase, resulting in a decrease in demand for municipal bonds by these significant buyers. While being dealt a severe blow, the municipal bond market nonetheless displayed a considerable amount of resiliency, continuing to furnish capital to municipalities for their many needs, and at the same time providing investors with tax-free income. With the same act eliminating most tax shelters, municipal bonds became the only game in town for individuals seeking to reduce their tax burden.

Once again, talk of tax reform has prophets of doom predicting the ruin of the municipal bond market. Various proposals drafted by members of Congress threaten to drastically change the U.S. income tax system as we know it today. The primary allure of municipal bonds under the current tax system is the tax-free status of the interest income received by investors on municipal obligations. (These bonds are often referred to by the investment community solely as tax-free bonds, evidencing the close tie between the municipal bond market and the income tax system.) Thus, anything that threatens to alter the current state of the tax code is sure to affect the ground rules associated with municipal bonds.

The proposals can be grouped into four categories:

1. a *flat tax*, virtually eliminating all deductions and at the same time lowering the marginal tax rates to *one* rate enjoyed by all taxpayers
2. the *elimination of the income tax system*, as we know it today, in favor of a national sales tax
3. the *outright taxation of interest* generated by municipal obligations (bonds)
4. the *elimination of taxation* on all interest and dividend income, creating a level playing field for all fixed-income securities

There is no doubt that the muni-market favors higher rather than lower tax rates. A flat tax—the lowering of marginal tax rates, coupled with an elimination of many deductions—would cause some damage to the market, as yields on existing municipal bonds are bid up and prices bid down as the market adjusts to the lower marginal tax rates. Interest rates on new issues would be higher as well, reflecting the lower tax rates. Much of this adjustment is already factored into the market's prices, as investors shun longer-term municipal bonds due to the uncertainty surrounding tax reform. There would, however, continue to be a definite tax advantage to owning municipal bonds under a flat tax system. *Overall, the implementation of a flat tax, contrary to popular belief, would not cripple the municipal bond market and is the most innocuous of the proposed changes!*

The remaining three proposals: the abolition of our current income tax system in favor of a national sales tax, or value-added tax (VAT); the outright taxation of municipal interest; and the elimination of taxation on all forms of interest income, if implemented, would impact the market more seriously, removing the tax advantages associated with municipal bonds. Prices of existing municipal securities could indeed drop precipitously, since new issues would come at significantly higher interest rates, or taxable rates. The municipal market, whose primary allure is its monopoly on providing investors with tax-free income would, in effect, be transformed into a taxable market, with a level playing field existing among all fixed-income markets. What good are tax-free bonds if there is no income tax?

Don't despair! First of all, the probability of the tax changes ending up as proposed are small, due to the plethora of special interest groups opposed to these changes. This is a fundamental problem with the promised revenue neutrality of many of these approaches, as well as the regressive nature of many of these plans. The most likely outcome will not be a major overhaul, but just a flatter tax, with marginal tax rates declining slightly, not at all ruinous to the municipal bond market. Second, the municipal bond market will undoubtedly survive even the most draconian of the proposals. While changes in the tax law would surely confound market participants, the municipal bond market nonetheless has an uncanny way of adjusting to changes in the environment. Remember, *municipal bonds are, and will always be, the primary way state and local governments raise money for their many needs.*

QUESTIONS AND ANSWERS

Q. Are municipal bonds solely for affluent investors?

A. No! One does not have to be affluent to enjoy the benefits of municipal bonds. While there is no denying that municipal bonds are purchased by those of the highest wealth levels, their appeal is much broader. Many middle class taxpayers looking to reduce their tax burden and increase their after-tax return find municipal bonds to be an integral part of their investment portfolios.

Using some basic arithmetic, one can ascertain whether municipal bonds should be considered as an investment vehicle. For example, an investor in the 35 percent tax bracket keeps only 65 percent (100 percent–35 percent) of every dollar earned on a taxable investment (such as a certificate of deposit or CD). Therefore, a 5 percent CD yields an investor in the 35 percent bracket only 3.25 percent (5 percent × 65 percent) in true after-tax dollars. A triple tax-free (exempt from federal, state, and local taxes) municipal bond yielding 4.25 percent involves an increase in income for this investor of a full 1 percent, as he gets to keep the full 4.25 percent. Remember, it is not the amount an investor earns but how much the investor keeps!

Q. Whenever I purchased municipal bonds in the past, they would be delivered to my home. My broker now tells me that most bonds issued today cannot be delivered. What's going on?

A. The vast majority of bonds are currently issued in book-entry form—a data entry on a computer. With book-entry bonds, purchasers cannot have their bonds delivered to their homes, but instead must rely on the custody statements issued by brokerage houses and banks. This system reduces paperwork for market participants, and eliminates lost or misplaced bonds. Old-time investors reluctant to hold their bonds in book-entry form may have no choice, because eventually all municipal bonds will probably be issued in this computerized form.

Q. What benefits will I realize by diversifying my municipal bond portfolio?

A. Diversifying means spreading out the risk over many issues and issuers resulting in less overall portfolio risk. In laymen's terms: Don't pull all your eggs in one basket! If one issue should default, it is comforting to know that only a small percentage of your bonds are involved. A guideline of no more than 5 to 10 percent of one's money in any one issue name may prove helpful. Investors should attempt to diversify geographically as well. However, when purchasing bonds issued by municipalities outside one's state of residency, the investor is forced to pay state and local taxes on the income generated from those bonds. The credit quality benefits derived from spreading the risk across state lines may far outweigh this financial penalty.

Q. What is a municipal bond fund and what benefits are derived by investing in one rather than purchasing individual bonds?

A. A municipal bond mutual fund is a pool of short-, intermediate-, or long-term municipal bonds—or a combination of all three—purchased by a manager on behalf of investors. When investors buy shares in a mutual bond fund they are, in effect, buying a cross-section of the overall portfolio, or a small slice of each bond in the fund. The interest on the municipal bonds that comprise the portfolio flows through tax free to the purchasers of the fund.

Municipal bond funds are ideal for those not interested in dedicating the time to learn and invest in specific tax-free bonds, and/or do not have sufficient funds to meet the minimum requirements of investing in single bonds. They offer professional management and instant diversification to municipal bond investors.

Q. What is a unit investment trust (UIT), and how does it differ from a municipal bond fund?

A. A municipal unit investment trust (UIT) in many ways is similar to a municipal bond fund. Investors, once again, are able to earn tax-exempt interest income without the need to learn about and purchase individual bonds. Through an investment of as little as $1,000, the investor receives the benefit of instant diversification, spreading out the risk among the many bonds in the portfolio. A sales charge of 4 to 5 percent is normally charged to the investor. The primary difference between a UIT and a mutual bond fund is that UITs are not managed. Once the trust is closed where all shares in the UIT are sold and the trust is in effect, sold out, the trading (buying or selling of any bonds) ceases. Bonds are thus purchased by the sponsor with the intent of holding them to maturity. Because there is no proactive management associated with unit investment trusts, once the trust is closed, expenses tend to be minimal, considerably less than with mutual bond funds.

Q. What factors will affect the salability of my municipal bonds?

A. There are several factors that will affect the marketability of one's municipal bonds.

1. *Block size.* The smaller the size of the block of bonds the less marketable. A wealthy individual selling a $500,000 block will receive a price that better approximates the bond's true value than one selling a block of $10,000.
2. *Quality and notoriety of bonds.* The higher quality, well-known names will demand a better bid that esoteric, low-quality issues.

3. *Market conditions.* Following negative market news, we can see the bid side on municipals—the price at which dealers will buy bonds—fall dramatically, and, in some cases, completely disappear, in which case bonds cannot be sold at any price.

It is strongly recommended that, if possible, the small investor use a buy-and-hold policy due to the relative inefficiency of the municipal bond market.

Q. Unlike Treasury securities, municipal bonds are not readily quoted in business periodicals. How can I be assured that I'm buying my municipal bonds at the most advantageous prices?

A. While the industry is moving toward better reporting and quoting of municipal bond prices, the fact remains that municipal bond price quotes are difficult, if not impossible, to uncover. It is therefore essential that municipal bond buyers shop around, soliciting offers from several dealers prior to purchasing a municipal bond. For high net worth individuals, a costly subscription to the Blue List, a daily publication of Standard & Poor's, listing many municipal bond offerings may prove a worthwhile investment.

Q. I have no tolerance for investment risk. While municipal bonds have an excellent repayment record, are there any municipal securities that have virtually no credit risk?

A. Yes, prerefunded municipal bonds may be just what the doctor ordered! Simply put, prerefunded bonds are municipal bonds that are no longer backed by the issuer but are instead backed normally by U.S. government securities. Therefore, the investor need not be concerned with the creditworthiness of the issuer. Prerefunded bonds should be rerated AAA by the rating agencies, attesting to the bonds' financial integrity and quality of those securities backing the bonds. If properly structured, owning a prerefunded bond is like having a tax-free Treasury bond.

GLOSSARY

Accrued interest amount of interest paid by the purchases of the security to the prior holder (seller) to compensate for interest earned since receiving the last payment.

After-tax yield return quoted on *discount municipal bonds* that reflect the fact that just the interest, and not the capital gains portion of the total return is tax free.

Alternative minimum tax (AMT) flat tax created by the IRS to penalize those taxpayers with a plethora of tax deductions in an attempt to make them pay their fair share. Basically, the AMT requires taxpayers to eliminate, or add back to taxable income, certain deductions that the tax code defines as preference items, and then recalculate their taxable income.

Arbitration situation in which an aggrieved investor goes before a panel of impartial mediators who render a binding decision regarding the complaint at hand.

Average life average time that a bond will be outstanding.

Basis point one one-hundredth of 1 percent (.01%)

Bearer bonds securities that do not contain information indicating the purchaser's name or address; whoever possesses the bond is deemed to be the owner.

Blue List current listing of municipal bonds owned by bond dealers who choose to advertise.

Bond anticipation note (BAN) short-term obligation issued in anticipation of an inevitable longer-term bond issuance.

Bond Buyer a trade newspaper, published daily, that contains comprehensive information on the municipal and Treasury bond market, including upcoming primary market sales, relevant news stories, and yield information.

Bond counsel attorney who gives the legal opinion attesting to the bond's tax-exempt status and compliance with current bond law.

Bond equivalent yield term used to compare T-bills—normally quoted in terms of a yield called the discount rate—to other non-discount, or coupon bearing, fixed-income instruments.

Bond indenture legal document that contains information regarding the legal rights of the bondholder, as well as terms and conditions of a bond offering.

Bond ratings grading system that compares the investment quality of various issuers.

Book-entry securities bonds that are not issued in physical form but are solely data entries on computer systems.

Brokers' broker brokers who do not maintain inventories, deal with the general public, or trade for their own accounts. Their job is to facilitate trading among the municipal bond dealer community.

Budget deficit insufficiency that occurs when the government spends more in a given year than it receives in taxes and other revenues.

Call feature agreement that gives the issuer the right to redeem bonds on a given date or dates prior to maturity at some specified price.

Certificate of participation (COP) municipal bond whose backing is derived from some form of lease payments.

Coupon rate stated rate of interest paid to the bondholder during the life of the bond.

Covenant a legal commitment on the part of the issuer. A rate covenant, or agreement, for instance, is a provision that requires the issuer to raise rates (user fees) in a sufficient amount to repay principal and interest to the bondholder.

Coverage ratio of a bond's net revenues to its total annual debt service; how many times the earnings of a project, minus operating expenses, cover the principal and interest payments to be made during the upcoming year.

Credit risk risk that involves the possibility of declining creditworthiness, or bankruptcy, on the part of an issuer.

Current yield yield or return calculated by dividing the coupon rate by the current price of the bond.

CUSIP number Committee Uniform Securities Identification Procedures number that is a universally known identification number given to virtually all municipal bonds.

Customer confirmation document the dealer is required to remit following the sale, or purchase, of any municipal security, verifying that a trade was consummated.

Dated date (Issue date) date on which the bonds begin accruing interest.

Debt service total of interest and principal payments to be made in a given year.

Default failure to repay interest and/or principal on a timely basis.

Derivative security security that gets its value from some underlying financial instrument.

Discount amount by which the price of a bond is less than its face value.

Discount rate (1) rate charged by the Federal Reserve for loans to member banks; (2) yield in which Treasury bills are normally quoted.

Dollar cost averaging buying a steady sum of a particular bond fund over a period of time, thus averaging out the overall price for shares of the fund. Dollar cost averaging normally results in a lower average cost per share.

Double-barreled bond bond with two or more types of backing. A common form is a revenue bond, which, in addition to the usual earmarked revenues, possesses the general obligation backing of the issuer.

Duration weighted average of when interest and principal is returned to the bond owner. It gives a more accurate picture of a bond's true maturity.

Dutch auction auction that differs from a conventional auction in that only one clearing rate—the rate at which all sellers sell and all buyers purchase the preferred stock at par, bringing supply and demand into equilibrium—is set. All participants who win shares in the auction thus receive the identical rate.

Federal funds rate interest rate charged when banks lend to each other overnight.

Federal Open Market Committee (FOMC) key decision-making body in the Federal Reserve system.

Fiscal policy use of government spending and/or taxation by the president and Congress to control the overall demand for goods and services by consumers, investors (in physical assets), and the government.

Flat tax tax that would eliminate all deductions while simultaneously lowering the marginal tax rates to *one* rate enjoyed by all taxpayers.

Futures contract contract that gives the investor the *right and obligation* to purchase or sell (take or make delivery) a commodity, stock, or, for our purposes, a bond, municipal or Treasury, at a specific price and date.

General obligation bonds (G-Os) bonds backed by a municipality's full faith and credit. Principal and interest are supported by the issuer's ability to levy taxes on real property, sales, and income.

Gross Domestic Product (GDP) sum of all goods and services produced within our nation's borders in a given year.

Index statistical compilation used to characterize a set of data.

Industrial development agency agency created specifically to promote industrial development in a particular area by allowing a corporate entity to borrow money at favorable tax-exempt interest rates.

Inflation rise in the overall level of prices.

Interest rate risk risk associated with rising interest rates and the accompanying decline in bond prices.

Investment bankers dealmakers who interface with the issuers, structuring bond deals that are ultimately sold to the investing public.

Investment grade term used to describe a bond rated Baa or better by Moody's and/or BBB or better by Standard & Poor's.

Issuer party borrowing the funds through *floating,* or selling, a bond issue.

Junk bonds high-yield bonds that are not creditworthy; they possess speculative elements that threaten their timely repayment.

Letter of credit bank's guarantee of timely repayment of interest and principal on a specific bond.

Load sales charge or commission paid to the sellers of various mutual funds.

Macroeconomics study that deals with the workings of the overall economy, including such topics as unemployment, inflation, the budget deficit, and foreign trade.

Marketability salability of a bond.

Maturity date date on which the bond is paid off and the debt ceases to exist.

Monetary policy policy that involves the controlling of the nation's money supply and short-term interest rates. It is administered by the Federal Reserve Bank (the Fed).

Municipal Assistance Corporation (MAC) corporation established by New York State to improve the overall economic condition of New York City, following the city's financial crisis in the 1970s.

Municipal auction preferred stock (MAPS) shares of *preferred stock* of a municipal bond fund. MAPS is a perpetual instrument (no ending maturity date), whose yield resets at various intervals such as 7 days, 28 days, etc., through a Dutch auction.

Municipal bond mutual fund pool of short-, intermediate-, or long-term municipal bonds, or a combination of all three, purchased by a manager on behalf of investors. When investors buy shares in a mutual bond fund, they are, in effect, buying a cross-section of the overall portfolio, a small slice of each bond in the fund.

Municipal Securities Rulemaking Board (MSRB) board created by Congress in the mid-1970s, to promulgate rules and regulations affecting both the municipal dealer and broker community.

National debt cumulative total of a nation's past budget deficits.

Net asset value term used in reference to dividing a municipal bond mutual fund's total worth by the number of shares outstanding.

Odd lot small block of bonds.

Official statement legal document prepared by the municipal issuer in conjunction with a financial advisor, consisting of extensive information about the municipality and the overall bond deal. This information includes a description of the municipal issuer, key demographic facts, the purpose of the bond issue, the security pledged to back the bonds, outstanding litigation, etc.

Par value face amount of the bond upon which the interest payments are figured.

Paying agent bank that makes the interest and principal payments to bondholders on behalf of the issuer.

Premium amount by which the price of a bond exceeds its face value.

Prerefunded bonds municipal bonds that are no longer backed by the issuer, but are instead backed by U.S. government securities. They no longer come due on the stated maturity date, but instead mature on a prior call date.

Present value term referring to a stated rate of interest that relates to a specific amount in the future (future value), and what it is worth today.

Primary market place where municipalities go to raise money for their many financial needs. When investors buy bonds in the primary market, they are, in effect, lending money to cities, towns, school districts, etc.

Principal amount amount the investor must pay for the bond, excluding the accrued interest.

Proceeds money received by an issuer following the sale of bonds to the investing public.

Put provision that allows the investor to relinquish bonds to the issuer, or a third party, and receive the principal some time prior to the bond's maturity. In effect, the put date can be viewed as the bonds real maturity date if the investor so wishes.

Registered bonds bonds, printed on paper, that are issued in physical form. The investor's name and address appear on the bond and are filed with the bond's paying agent—the bank that makes the interest and principal payments to the holders of the bonds—so that interest is mailed to the customer along with the principal repayment when the bond matures.

Revenue anticipation note (RAN) short-term obligation issued in anticipation of some form of revenue other than taxes, such as state aid.

Revenue bond bond structure that involves securing bonds with revenues generated from a specific project. Revenue, rather than taxing power, associated with G-Os, is therefore pledged to repay bondholders.

Secondary market (resale market) market where investors go to sell their municipal bonds, or to purchase other investors' existing, or used, bonds.

Settlement date date on which the bonds must be paid for. Unless otherwise specified, settlement in the municipal market is three business days following the trade date (Trade + 3, T+3).

Sinking fund fund set aside by the issuer to retire, or call in, a certain amount of debt each year.

Spread total profit hoped to be realized by dealers when underwriting bonds.

Super Sinkers bonds that involve a unique financial structure that mandates the issuer to use all funds from early mortgage prepayments of a particular bond issue to retire (call in) bonds of a specific *maturity* of that same issue; normally associated with single-family housing issues.

Swap a strategy that involves the sale of a currently held bond and the simultaneous purchase of another bond to achieve a desired goal.

Syndicate group of dealers that join forces for the purpose of purchasing a bond issue from a municipality.

Take-and-pay contracts contracts that are involved primarily with public power bonds, and that require participants to pay for power only when available.

Take-or-pay contracts contracts that are involved primarily with public power bonds, that require participants to pay for their share of power costs, whether or not power is ever produced.

Tax anticipation note (TAN) short-term obligation issued in anticipation of future tax collections.

Taxable equivalent yield formula that enables an investor to compare the yield on tax-exempt securities to comparable tax bonds. Taxable Equivalent Yield = Tax-Free Yield / (100% − Marginal Tax Rate).

Tax-exempt money market mutual fund fund that can be viewed as a tax-fee checking or savings account and is managed, but not guaranteed, to maintain a $1.00 per share net asset value.

Term bond longest maturity of a new issue that normally makes up the bulk of the bonds that comprise the issue.

Trade date date on which the transaction is initiated and confirmed.

Traders individuals who take positions and make markets—agree to buy and sell—in various securities.

Treasury securities IOUs that are backed by the full faith and credit of the U.S. government.

Trustee a fiduciary, normally a bank, whose primary responsibility is protecting the bondholder by compelling the issuer to abide by the terms of the bond contract.

Underwriting act of bringing new issues to market. It involves a dealer firm or firms purchasing a bond issue—lending funds to a municipality—and subsequently selling the issue to investors.

Unit investment trust (UIT) diversified municipal bond portfolio. Units are sold to investors who, in effect, are buying a cross-section, or slice of each bond, of the portfolio. The primary difference between a UIT and a mutual bond fund is that UITs are not managed.

Variable-rate demand bond (lower floater) long-term tax-exempt municipal bond that is converted by a dealer firm into a short-term security.

Yield curve graph that depicts the relationship between the maturity of a bond and the interest rates offered on the bond.

Yield to maturity internal rate of return on a bond.

Zero coupon bond bond that does not pay the investor interest each year; rather, the investor purchases the bonds at a discount to face value (price less than) and receives only one single (bullet) payment at maturity when the bonds are redeemed for the face value.

INDEX